FRED SIRIEIX moved to the UK in the summer of 1992. He worked in senior front-of-house positions at landmark London restaurants, including Le Gavroche, Sartoria, Brasserie Roux and Galvin at Windows at the London Hilton, where he worked as general manager until 2019. In the last decade, Sirieix has been a constant presence on our screens across a variety of channels – the hit show *First Dates*, *Remarkable Places to E*… *ackmasters* on Channel 4; *My Mi*… *enu* and *Ultimate Wedding* … *Road Trip* on ITV … and Gino D'A… *elebrity … Get Me* … spare time, he set up the … urse, an initiative to adapt prison … professional kitchens run by inmates.

SERIOUSLY BRITISH

FRED SIRIEIX

B L O O M S B U R Y   P U B L I S H I N G
LONDON • OXFORD • NEW YORK • NEW DELHI • SYDNEY

BLOOMSBURY PUBLISHING
Bloomsbury Publishing Plc
50 Bedford Square, London, WC1B 3DP, UK
Bloomsbury Publishing Ireland Limited,
29 Earlsfort Terrace, Dublin 2, D02 AY28, Ireland

BLOOMSBURY, BLOOMSBURY PUBLISHING and the Diana logo are trademarks of Bloomsbury Publishing Plc

First published in Great Britain 2024
This edition published 2025

A catalogue record for this book is available from the British Library

ISBN: HB: 978-1-5266-7869-0; PB: 978-1-5266-7919-2;
eBook: 978-1-5266-7921-5; ePDF: 978-1-5266-7920-8

2 4 6 8 10 9 7 5 3 1

Typeset by Newgen KnowledgeWorks Pvt. Ltd., Chennai, India
Printed and bound in Great Britain by CPI Group (UK) Ltd,
Croydon CR0 4YY

MIX
Paper | Supporting responsible forestry
FSC www.fsc.org FSC® C013604

To find out more about our authors and books visit
www.bloomsbury.com and sign up for our newsletters
For product safety related questions contact productsafety@bloomsbury.com

To Fruitcake, Andrea and
Matteo Lucien, Mum and Dad

CONTENTS

Introduction

I stood on the deck of a P&O ferry with a one-way ticket in my hand watching France recede into the distance. I was twenty years old and it was the summer of 1992. I had a friend who worked at the famous two-Michelin-starred restaurant La Tante Claire in Chelsea, and he said there was a job waiting for me. I didn't need to think about it – I'd be starting the life that I'd fantasised about for ages. My mum was angry with me, not least because I'd left France before I'd even received my exam results for my professional *baccalauréat* in catering. I knew she wanted me to go on to university but I wasn't interested in that. I wanted to live my life. I wanted to be free.

I had been determined to live in the UK for several years. Beyond that, I didn't know what to expect. I certainly didn't imagine that, ten years later, I'd be buying a flat in Peckham, terrified at the prospect of a £472-a-month mortgage. And now, thirty-two years after that ferry trip, I'm still here, having fallen in love with the place, put down roots in south-east London and raised two beautiful, incredible children.

It all began for me on an exchange with an English family in Stratford-upon-Avon in the summer of 1986. I was fourteen. On the first day, I was handed a plastic box. 'Here's your lunch, Fred,' the kind mother said with a smile. I smiled back but I was confused. My English wasn't brilliant but I was fairly sure she'd just told me that this was lunch, in a box. When she was out of the room, I put the box on the table and unfastened the clip. There were four compartments, one each for a sandwich, a packet of crisps, a tangerine and a chocolate bar. I stared at it. I'm sure it wasn't that dissimilar to the scene in *Pulp Fiction* when Vincent Vega opens the mystery briefcase and remains motionless for several seconds, completely transfixed by its contents.

Now, you might assume that French people would look upon such a thing with disdain, maybe even disgust, but to a teenager from Limoges in France's rural heart, it was a revelation. Before me was a palette of unexpected colours and flavours. We were barely fifty miles from the coast of France, but this might as well have been another planet. Where was my *entrée*, *plat du jour* and *dessert*? Where was my cheese course? Maybe this was the 'Anarchy in the UK' that the Sex Pistols had been shouting about.

The bread – it was so lovely and soft, like a welcoming little pillow. That first salt and vinegar crisp was a taste explosion. And it didn't matter which order you ate your lunch in. It didn't matter what time you ate it. No one was watching you. You could do what you liked. Sprinkle those salt and vinegar beauties inside your sandwich if you want to. *Vive la révolution!*

It took some getting used to. In France, meals are sacred. They're ritualistic, almost religious occasions. Every single lunch or dinner is a three-course meal with wine. Lunch is at twelve o'clock and dinner at seven. In our home, it was always my job to set the table, partly because my brother Pierre systematically seemed to be taking a tactical shit just at the precise moment that help was needed. I'd lay out the cutlery for our three courses, line up the glasses for wine and water, place the baguette properly on the table (on its back, never the other way round as that is disrespectful), slide the butter into its dish, position the salt and pepper pots and the mustard and make sure there was a properly folded napkin at each place setting. And then we sat down before my mother served the first course. In France, you always wait for the food; the food doesn't wait for you. There'd always be cheese after our main course before my mum brought out some kind of expertly crafted tart, mousse or soufflé. After that we'd have yogurt. French people always have yogurt. Then we'd clear the table. And that was just a regular lunch at home, any day of the week. Then you did the same again for dinner. Every day.

Everything seemed so much more flexible in the UK; and at a time in my life when I was beginning to question how things are done and rebel, it presented itself as the land of opportunity. I told myself that the next time I returned to these shores, it would be for good. All this was running through my head as a twenty-year-old chugging ever closer to the famous white cliffs surrounding the old port of Dover. I'd spent most of the journey on deck, looking directly ahead towards them, my two suitcases either side of me. I found my way to Dover Priory train station and then to London.

After getting off at Victoria station, things happened really quickly. I went to the restaurant, was shown around and introduced to everyone, then I was presented with the rota on the wall. Monday–Friday FRED ON, it said. Suddenly everything became real. I was then taken to a bedsit, met the landlady and paid my deposit. All at once, the flurry of activity ended. I was standing alone in silence, holding a key. I was tingling all over.

The bedsit was in Pimlico, a strangely down-at-heel neighbourhood given that it was only just north of the Thames and so close to all the sights, but I really liked it. I worked out that I'd be earning £812 a month after tax. It's funny how figures like that never leave your head. Likewise, I remember that the bedsit cost £50 a week and I was working Monday to Friday, so, unlike folks following a similar path today, I found myself with disposable income and the time to enjoy it. I spent most of it in restaurants, cafés, pubs and nightclubs. And for good reason.

Growing up in France came with its benefits, for sure – that sense of rigour and ritual taught me self-discipline and self-motivation, and I knew what good food tasted like because we ate fresh seasonal food all the time. But while you're eating a wonderful variety of food, that's where the variety ends – you're always eating French food with French people. In London, however, I found restaurants of every cultural origin you can imagine. And it absolutely blew my mind. I had my first ever Chinese, Indian and Thai meals in London. I could have a Greek breakfast, a Lebanese lunch and a Nepali dinner all in the same day if I wanted to. There was so much choice. There were so many flavours. I spent my first few weeks walking around with my eyes wide open like one of the kids who'd just seen the inside of Willy Wonka's chocolate factory.

It wasn't just the food that was exciting and varied. One of the first places I wanted to see was Piccadilly Circus. I'd heard it was the beating heart of the capital – the bright lights, the neon signs, the red buses carrying people this way and that. I took my first trip on the Tube to get there, and I was instantly captivated by the variety of people next to me. There was a builder reading the *Sun*, a female Asian student, a City gent wearing a pinstriped suit and me – a young French guy.

I enjoyed taking the bus even more than the Tube. It was partly because I loved the iconic red Routemasters but also because it was another facet of the freedom I'd yearned for back in France. With that long pole at the back of the bus that was open to the elements, you could jump on and off whenever you wanted, even when the bus was moving. You could chase after the bus, grab for the pole and swing yourself in. And you were rewarded for it with the best view in the city – watching the world go by while you're holding on to that pole. It felt like I'd been transported into *Singing in the Rain*.

It was all so far removed from the land of '*les Rosbifs*', the French stereotype about British cuisine that has been repeated for generations. It's just one of several stereotypes about the UK that you hear in France. Like British wine being undrinkable, or that Britain is ugly, rainy and grey with nothing worth visiting beyond London and Edinburgh. Or that British people aren't romantic or stylish, or that they're too reserved and meek. In the thirty-two years that I've lived in the UK – longer than I've lived in France – I've found the truth to be very different.

This is my love letter to the UK.

1

'Britain is Ugly and Grey'

I completely understand why the Vikings invaded England in the ninth century. The countryside is so green and the landscape is so beautiful. The Vikings would have seen the coasts on their pillaging raids, but it's when they sailed inland along the waterways that they would have seen the rolling hills and ancient forests. That's when they must have thought *Wow – everything's going to grow here!* So they broke a raiding tradition that spanned generations and set up camp here. They were led by the sons of Ragnar Lothbrok, whose name translates, amazingly, as 'Hairy Pants'. But it was no laughing matter for the Anglo-Saxons, because by 871, the Vikings had wiped out the rulers of three of the four Anglo-Saxon kingdoms. Alfred, King of Wessex, was the only one to survive, and he did that by the skin of his teeth. It didn't look good for him, but Brits love an underdog almost as much as a double entendre, and Alfred took down Hairy Pants at the Battle of Edington in 878. Just over fifty years later, in 929, King Æthelstan united the four kingdoms (Wessex, East Anglia, Mercia and Northumbria), and England was born.

I've been lucky enough to travel to every corner of the UK, and have been to some remarkable places, from the pastel-coloured beach huts on Southwold

Promenade at dawn to the picture-postcard beauty of the Lake District. I've discovered the tranquillity of the north coast of Northern Ireland, the magnificence of Pembrokeshire and how much the New Forest reminds me of the ancient woods back home. I've done some things I never imagined doing, like competing in the Highland Games and trying truffles that were grown in Monmouthshire. I've even become a gardener (I still can't quite understand how that's happened). It's fair to say that these islands have truly captured my heart.

My first summer in the UK while I was working at La Tante Claire, I drove down to Cornwall with some friends. I remember it well because we took the A303 and it was the first time I'd seen Stonehenge. You never forget something like that. The landscape begins to flatten out and you find yourself on a plain with stunning views of the countryside in every direction. Then suddenly, without any notice, you go up a little hill and the world's most famous prehistoric monument appears just on your right. You only appreciate the scale of the site when you approach the stones. And then you can't help but wonder who built it and why they did – and how on earth they shifted the stones there because all you've seen for the last forty-five minutes of driving is undulating fields and hedgerows without a rock in sight. The fact that Stonehenge was built to align with the sun on the winter and summer solstices is staggering. If you stand in the centre of the monument, the sun on the summer solstice rises just over the 'Heel' stone, the largest stone there. During the winter solstice, the sun sets between the narrow gap of the tallest 'trilithon' (two vertical stones linked by a horizontal lintel). The more you learn about Stonehenge, the more your mind is blown. After that first visit, I started imagining the people who built it, wandering around exactly where I was 5,000 years ago. It was almost like you could feel them all around the stones. It made the place feel very crowded with the voices of the past.

After that amazing stop, we carried on to Cornwall, which felt like such a stark contrast to the busy London restaurant I was working in. Cornwall is so unspoiled. The roads are narrow, the villages are quaint with their grey granite cottages and the coast is so rugged. You feel far away and you can switch off. We found a hostel in Newquay, and I'll never forget seeing Fistral Beach for the first time. We were walking along a street of backpacker hostels and then suddenly saw this huge, horseshoe-like bay with the breaking waves in the distance. It was a breathtaking sight. I enjoy walking and we found a beautiful coastal walk along the cliff path from Newquay up to Watergate Bay, a stunning two-mile-long beach with golden sands and dramatic cliffs. Being up on the clifftops, the wind on your face, the sound of the breaking waves and the taste of salt on your lips, is an immersive, elemental experience. Cornwall's all about that to me. It's so invigorating.

It's wonderful that there are so many sides to Cornwall. You've got the spectacular coasts, but you've also got the beautiful green countryside, which makes you calm, peaceful and serene. You see several different landscapes in one walk, and then you've got the incredible brick chimneys rising out of the moorland, a vestige of Cornwall's industrial past when it was providing roughly two-thirds of global demand for copper and tin. Against the backdrop of rugged cliffs and wild moorland, it does feel like a very romantic landscape. Then you get these beautiful subtropical gardens originally created by the Victorian mine owners.

Some of the old mines are further inland and nature's reclaimed them, so you find these unexpected valleys full of greenery. Other former mining sites have been repurposed into museums or steam railway lines, but probably the most remarkable is the Eden Project. The sheer scale and diversity of it is mind-blowing. When you come out of the Eden Project, you feel more intelligent than when you went in. It's another example of that unique Cornish experience – turning a corner and then being amazed by an unexpected multi-sensory experience.

And then you've got the local Cornish gastronomy, which is really impressive. Paul Ainsworth at No. 6 in Padstow is a special place. It's this gorgeous Georgian town house just off the harbour, and I'd say it was one of the best meals I've had in the UK. The food is delicious and really showcases the local produce, as does the sparkling wine from Camel Valley, which was excellent, but the hospitality – which always matters a lot to me – is pitch-perfect. You leave afterwards having had not just a great meal, but an amazing experience. It also feels really good to support the local economy.

Cornwall isn't the only coastal region I enjoy spending time in. Devon is on my list of favourites too. When I came to the UK in the early nineties, it felt like everyone was suggesting going down to Cornwall in the summer, Newquay especially. No one was talking about Devon. It somehow felt like Cornwall's overshadowed little brother, and I only really explored it properly a decade later. When I first visited South Devon, and I learned that it was nicknamed the English Riviera (after the French Riviera – the south-eastern coast of France), I wasn't surprised. It does look similar, with its Mediterranean feel, palm trees, pine forests, promenades and sunny stretches of sand. What I didn't know was that, among Brits, it became a joke term for a while after John Cleese described Torquay as the 'English Riviera' in the fantastic *Fawlty Towers*. Brits are just too self-deprecating – South Devon is actually really beautiful. But Brits compare it to the French Riviera, give a wry smile, and think *this is as good as it gets*. However, if you see it through my eyes, and you look at it for what it is, you think 'This is beautiful!' It depends how you see things. If you're always looking over to your neighbour with 'the grass is always greener' mentality then you're never going to be happy. Incidentally, I'm really proud of my grass and it looks better than my neighbour's, which I like to wind him up about.

There's an excellent larder there in Devon with fantastic fish and seafood, cheeses, ice cream, fudge, orchard fruits and cider. Everything you need for a good holiday. Dartmouth is a wonderful vision of Old England to me. It's a stunning place with the view across the water over to Kingswear, the naval college to your left and Dartmouth Castle (another castle built to keep the French away!) to your right. What makes it even more glorious is the rolling green countryside that surrounds it. One particular favourite place of mine is the Seahorse restaurant in Dartmouth run by Mitch Tonks and his son Ben, who's now the head chef. It's an absolutely incredible seafood restaurant which I was introduced to by my friend Angela Hartnett. It's a family-run place, it's intimate, the kitchen is on show and it's all about the quality of the fresh fish and shellfish, the excellence of the cooking and the fantastically welcoming hospitality. It almost feels like you've been invited into their house. It's also really well priced so you're getting five-star quality food at normal prices in a stunning setting. It's what the Brits refer to as 'understated luxury'. It's a very special restaurant.

Right, let's address the elephant in the room. All this talk of Cornwall and Devon and I know what you're thinking. Is he a jam first or a cream first guy? Cream of course. Here's why. Cream is like butter – it's a fat. When you are buttering your toast, as we all do around the breakfast table in the UK, you put the butter on first and then the jam second. The same principle should apply for scones – it's logical! I rest my case. Of course, in life, you can do whatever you want and if you prefer the other way around, I'm not going to judge you.

I absolutely love that when you go down to the coast, people still go to the beach even when it's hammering down with rain. They're still doing things that everyone all over the world does on the beach – making sandcastles and having ice creams – but they're happy to do them while getting soaked. That's what I think of when I see the words 'Keep calm and carry on'. It was the same during the Blitz. The bombs are falling but the Brits will get on with it. As long as there's a nice cup of tea and a biscuit to dunk into it, they'll be all right. The same mentality continues, eighty years after the end of World War II. We're drenched in rain, but we're getting on with it. Keep smiling.

This doesn't happen in France! If it's raining, the only creatures you'll find on the beach are seagulls. A friend of mine told me recently that you could replace all the questions on the British citizenship test with just one: have you had a barbecue in the rain? Let me tell you: if I've planned a barbecue, it's happening, come hell or high water. My dad wouldn't dream of such an abomination, nor would anyone in France. To be honest, I like barbecuing in the rain because it goes against the grain – for the French, anyway. So let's keep calm and carry on grilling those sausages, come rain, sun or snow.

I've got to know the West Country much better since 2020 because I took a trip there with Michel Roux Jr for *Remarkable Places to Eat.* Bristol is his favourite place in the UK and I can see why. It's got so much character and you never know what you're going to find around the next corner. I certainly wasn't expecting to find the oldest heated public swimming pool in the country down a residential street right next to a pub. Built in 1849, it used to be called Clifton Victoria Baths. The place fell into disrepair by 1990 and there was talk of knocking it down and making way for a block of flats, but it was restored in the 2000s. It was turned into an open-air pool, renamed Clifton Lido and it now looks spectacular. It's an urban oasis. You don't even need to be a member – you can pay for a swim and breakfast as part of a package deal. It was Christmas-time and Michel had brought along a pair of festive swimming trunks for me, so

I looked like Santa in Speedos. Apparently you're not allowed to dive in, which is why Michel started to get into the pool like a grandad, going gingerly down the steps. I didn't have time for any of that, so I dived in. After all, we were in Bristol – the rebel city.

On Michel's recommendation, we went to a fantastic French bistro called Little French in the Bristol neighbourhood of Westbury Park, run by husband-and-wife duo Freddy and Nessa Bird. A British chef serving French bistro food to Michel must have been daunting but they did a brilliant job and the service was incredible. We also visited the Newt, a beautiful boutique hotel in a Palladian red-gold limestone country house about thirty miles south of Bristol. It was spectacular. I wasn't expecting to find that they made their own cider, a drink with a special place in my heart. As a boy growing up in rural France, autumn was always a special season. Lots of villages near Limoges hosted festivals come September to celebrate the heritage and humble produce of our region. I have the most wonderful memories of these niche festivals, like '*La fête de la châtaigne*', where I would gorge on roasted chestnuts, and '*La fête de la pomme*', which we'd come back from carrying bottles of cider and fresh apple juice. I drank cider for the first time, aged six or seven, with my grandfather in his cellar, where he kept the good stuff. It was very dark, covered in cobwebs and had a very low ceiling and a dodgy floor basically just made of clay. But he loved that space – that's where he had hams hanging up, potatoes, racks of wine and his prized hand tools.

I've also got to know Bath very well because of filming series 10 of *First Dates* there. Bath is a beautiful city. It's actually the only British city (in its entirety) which is designated a UNESCO World Heritage Site. Everything's made of these honey-coloured old stones and it's reminiscent of some of the old villages of France and Italy. But it's actually quintessentially British, the architecture, the way the stones are carved, the names of the streets, the boutique shops and the beautiful greenery and parkland. I love that it's a city of different time periods, with its Roman ruins, medieval cathedral and Georgian splendour. It's a wonderful place to walk around. Much of the centre is pedestrianised so you catch snippets of conversations in the street. It makes you feel very relaxed, conjuring up the perfect atmosphere so you can soak up the remarkable history all around you.

One afternoon, after we'd finished shooting an episode of *First Dates*, I went for a walk. I ended up in a park and was surprised to see that there was a keenly contested *pétanque* tournament going on. I watched for a little bit and then a couple of the players recognised me and invited me over to join them for a game. It was amazing. Everybody was English but they were playing French music from the 1960s, 70s and 80s. I knew all the tracks. I could sing all the songs. Every single word. I stayed for a couple of hours playing *pétanque* with a bunch of lovely guys and had a few drinks. I lost though! I couldn't believe it. Maybe I should have challenged them to a game of cricket after.

I fell in love with the vibrant and unique charm of Peckham and ended up buying a place there. Once I'd gone south of the river, I couldn't go back north – I realised that I'd found my tribe as a south Londoner. Peckham was diverse, vibey, inclusive and, most importantly, real, and all those things made it beautiful to me. My roots were in rural working-class France, but I chose to put down new roots in the urban, working-class environment of Peckham. I loved the local restaurant scene and the shops. I loved the fact that a local artist sculpted the trunk of a fallen plane tree into a totem pole in 2013. And I love that I fell in love with my partner, Fruitcake, there.

I bought a flat there for £70k with a £3k deposit, and my mortgage was £472 a month. I sold it a few years later and bought a house. Like I said, I always remember figures, especially the cost of that flat, because I was shitting myself the first time I saw it! I've always been very careful with money. I grew up hearing the fable about the grasshopper and the ant, where the grasshopper is partying all summer and then realises that it's getting cold and he's in trouble. Meanwhile, the ant's been sensible and thought ahead. But he's got a good heart and lets the grasshopper in when he knocks on the ant's door with his tail between his legs.

Setting down roots in the UK made me want to make a difference here. I'd always been an advocate of helping disadvantaged young people but it wasn't until around the time that my daughter Andrea was born that I started to turn thoughts into action. During that time I was cycling into Central London from Peckham and I was being diverted almost every day around the Old Kent Road by police tape. A lot of young people were losing their lives to knife crime. And then I remember reading a very moving article on this eighteen-year-old guy called Alex Rose, whose friend had died in his arms. His friend's death had a profound effect on him and after that tragic incident he took a different path, launching a campaign to stop violence. Sometimes, all it takes is one wrong turn and your life can become very dark very quickly. In 2008, after meeting him, I decided to start a scheme to help underprivileged young people, who had made bad decisions or felt like there was no other way out for them, to gain professional qualifications so they could work in hotels, restaurants and bars.

Nine years later, I founded the charity The Right Course. My plan was to teach prison inmates how to work in and run a restaurant. We did that by transforming the existing staff canteen into a fully functioning professional kitchen staffed by the inmates. They train and work as front of house, as baristas and as chefs, and the customers in our prison restaurants are the prison staff. So we adapt our prices to encourage them to eat there rather than bringing in their own packed lunch. As with every restaurant, you've got to instil a sense of camaraderie between the kitchen and the front-of-house team, but unlike other restaurants, you've also got to create a relationship between the restaurant staff and the customers (the prison staff). So the dynamic is unique. Inmates need to look after the prison staff and the prison staff need to be happy being looked after by the inmates. It's all about trust. While the inmates are gaining qualifications, we're arranging interviews for them with potential employers so that when they're released, they've got a job. Adult offenders have a reoffending rate of between 12 and 50 per cent depending on the nature of the crime, but we know from research that if you have a job, keep in contact with your friends and family and have a place to live, you're far less likely to reoffend.

Prisons are never pretty places, but we have a team of designers working pro bono for us who combine functionality and beauty in our restaurant designs. We need the restaurant to be the best it can be, because we're not just serving a good meal – we're providing a path towards a law-abiding life. If you've got an aesthetically pleasing and well-thought-out restaurant, it has a subconsciously positive impact on everyone. If the workers are happy, it's easier to make the customers happy. And if the customers are happy, it positively impacts the workers. You start a virtuous circle, which is consistent with our vision for the charity. Our aim is two-fold: to reduce reoffending and to secure employment upon release. A job is a gateway to a more positive path. Also, what better place is there to begin a virtuous circle than a prison? Seeing the prisoners working hard to perfect what they do and enjoying it, while smiling and laughing with the prison staff completely transforms the atmosphere of a prison. It makes you realise how much the people make the place, and how you can find beauty in the most unexpected settings.

After HMP Isis in 2017, the prisons we've opened restaurants in so far are Wormwood Scrubs in west London (2021), Berwyn in North Wales (2023) and Lincoln (also 2023), and three more are set to open in 2024. Every governor in every prison is responsible for their budget. They can get a grant for projects like this through various government departments and we've had some donors chip in. It's a very worthy cause. We have a couple of core costs like a CEO, who deals with day-to-day management, and an operations manager to check and control quality, but that's it. We're completely transparent. Any money we have goes straight into the charity. We definitely don't spend our cash and donations on brainstorming retreats at Soho Farmhouse! I find it really rewarding and it gives me a goal. It's very satisfying to be able to make a difference and create opportunities for others. And while it's been quite successful so far, I recognise that there's a long way to go.

For this scheme to work in the long term, it has to be done large scale. And that's why I'm aiming to open a restaurant in every prison in the UK. I'd like to find a way of adapting it to try and help the bigger problem, which is why people are ending up in prison in the first place. A lot of people in prison were excluded from school. This can happen for all sorts of reasons. Sometimes people can just be victims of circumstance, and society can give up on you. But no one wins when people go to prison. We're all part of society, and if we want it to improve, we've got to change things. Education doesn't stop when you leave school – it carries on for the whole of your life. For me, there are only two ways you can go as you age: either you turn into vinegar or a beautiful Bordeaux. And the choice is up to you.

As you know, there are a number of things about the UK that I loved immediately, like the freedom of a lunch box as a teenager compared to the rigid formality of a three-course lunch. And then there are the things I didn't think I'd like in a million years that have crept up and surprised me. I grew up watching both of my parents lovingly tending the garden at our house in France – they still do – but I could not have given a monkey's about gardening. So how has going to the Chelsea Flower Show become one of the highlights of my year?

I love attention to detail and working hard. And you can't get a finer example of both of these things than one of the show gardens at Chelsea. When you look at the site a few days before the event, it's basically a big lawn with a few bare patches. Fast-forward a week and it's staggering how much is achieved in such a short space of time. For me, the Chelsea Flower Show and the garden in general is about beauty. It's the art of creating a feast not only for the eyes, but for all of the senses. The way all the flowers and colour come together, and the way they blossom at different times is a feat of engineering, planning and wizardry. I know from my own experience that ensuring your garden is always in bloom is tough – there's an art to it. You've really got to apply yourself and be curious. We have garden centres and plant nurseries in France, but the British approach to gardening is on another level. People are really proud about their gardens. They are in France too, but here, it's deeper. It's almost like the passion goes all the way down to their roots. I think part of it is because you have to be patient. You plant things now and in several months you're rewarded with flowers. I think it's very suited to the English psyche and the idea that patience and persistence pays off.

The first thing I do after I wake up is have a coffee and wander outside with the secateurs, in my socks and sandals. I even name my plants. I'm like a true Brit with my lawn. I look at it, scanning for any sign of a weed or imperfection, and if there is one, I'm straight out there. Every week I cut the grass and I do it with such pride. I love it to be neat, making sure that the lawnmower lines are all straight. My aim is to make my lawn like a golf green: smooth, flat and even. I do the edges with a pair of scissors. The rest of the garden I want to look like a show garden at the Chelsea Flower Show. I'm always working on it. It's never-ending. But the lawn is the biggest part of your garden and it has to be perfect so that it elevates everything else. If you've got a beautiful lawn, you're halfway there. My dad loves his roses, but his lawn? – it's despicable. If I was trying to soften the blow like Brits do, I'd call it a 'laissez-faire lawn'. The grass is greener this side of the Channel, Dad.

Maybe that's why I even enjoy the rain now. There's something beautiful about the rain and the shades of grey in the sky. It makes the garden look alive and smell divine. It's going to make my flowers grow. If I had to wait for a blue sky to appear and the sun to come out in order to be happy, I'm not going to be happy that often. So I make the most of what's in front of me. As I'm writing this, in March 2024, there's going to be an explosion of colour in a few weeks in my garden and I can't wait. My favourite season is definitely spring. It's getting warmer, the green shoots in the garden are showing, the leaves are starting to appear and the spring flowers are opening up, but the thing I love the most is that the days are longer. You can wake up at 6 a.m. in late April and it's daytime. I sleep with the windows open and the curtains open and our bedroom's east-facing so the rays of sunlight kiss the walls and wake me up gently. The birds are starting to sing and I love that sense of tranquillity before the world wakes up. I miss that time of year when it goes but then I look forward to the next year.

Another thing about the UK that surprised me was how much the New Forest reminds me of the area that I'm from in France. Only, it has all these historic, uniquely British quirks. The first time I went there I was amazed to see dozens of beautiful wild ponies. *What the hell?!* There are around 5,000 of them wandering about, as they have been for around 2,000 years, and technically they're owned (and cared for) by the 'commoners' – the people who live in the New Forest. The whole area was declared a royal forest for hunting deer in 1079 by William the Conqueror, although this didn't quite go to plan, as his son, William II, was killed by an arrow meant for a stag not far from Brockenhurst in 1100. There's a stone – the Rufus Stone – that marks the spot. Locals weren't allowed to hunt, graze their livestock or even forage the forest until a document called 'The Charter of the Forest' was signed in 1217, and they've been proud of it ever since. Most of the rights are still in effect today. One of them is called 'pannage' – the right to let pigs roam for sixty days starting in mid-September so they can forage for acorns and beech nuts, which are poisonous to cows and ponies. They'll also hoover up anything else going, like fallen apples and chestnuts. And your lunch if you're not looking.

My friend, TV presenter and fresh-produce expert Chris Bavin took me to see the New Forest in 2021, where he'd spent many happy holidays as a kid. I discovered some amazing places like Lime Wood, near Lyndhurst – a special place for a special occasion. It's a beautiful stucco-fronted Georgian country house that's been turned into a stylish hotel, spa, restaurant and everything else I could want for a weekend retreat. The Pig in Brockenhurst, in the heart of the New Forest, is an incredible hotel and restaurant where they build their menu around what they can grow in their kitchen garden. They keep chickens so they've got fresh eggs and they even grow their own mushrooms. Anything they have to bring in, they source within a twenty-five-mile radius of the restaurant. The pigs that have been fattening up on the pannage are butchered, salted and cooked in the winter, and the restaurant staff roast the meat in a wood-fired oven. There's other amazing stuff going on as well, like at the New Forest Smokery, where they farm brown trout and rainbow trout, smoke it and turn it into pâté. Not what this Frenchman was expecting but a pleasant surprise! The New Forest is a great place to wander around. When I'm not working or exercising, I love taking time as it comes and living slowly.

Walking around the Kent Downs is one of my favourite things. It's remarkable that you can be half an hour from London and not come across another soul for miles. You're just surrounded by nature. I'm always heading off on different walks and it's taken me all over Kent and Sussex. One of my favourite things to chance upon is a game of cricket on a village green. I've sat down for hours on a bench completely captivated by this elaborate game. Even if you don't understand the rules, you can still follow it. The games I've seen usually involve a crowd of older Brits, and everything seems very ordered and quiet – until someone's out. Then suddenly these reserved, shy Brits are all jumping around, shouting and hugging each other. Brits just need the right place and they'll let their hair down!

I have very fond memories of going to Lord's to watch a Test match. There's nothing quite like cricket, staying there all day and drinking a lovely cool pint at the height of summer while you're watching the game unfold. As I was there, I realised that there were certain similarities between cricket and gardening. You wait around for ages for something to happen, but when it does – *c'est magnifique*! I've said it before and I'll say it again: Brits are patient folks. It's why queuing is perfectly suited to the British mindset. Persistence pays off and you need both in spades for gardening and cricket. At the cricket, you've even got a nice break for lunch and tea – it's all very civilised, except for the fact that by the close of play, you realise you've had a couple of glasses of wine over lunch and a couple of pints of beer and it's only 6.30. Drinking aside, it's the most relaxing sport I've ever watched. Everyone's in a good mood. And you get to meet and have fascinating conversations with the people around you.

Kent, the Garden of England, is where I now live and I love it – the countryside is so beautiful. I went to Sissinghurst Castle Garden for the first time a few years ago when Fruitcake surprised me with a visit there and it blew me away. You arrive and suddenly there's this Elizabethan tower that makes you feel like Rapunzel's about to let down her hair. Vita Sackville-West, the author and member of the famous 'Bloomsbury Group', bought it with her husband, the diplomat and author Harold Nicolson, in 1930. Because of the rules of primogeniture, she couldn't inherit Knole, her family home, from her father, Baron Sackville, when he died in 1928. Back then, Sissinghurst was a sprawling farm with some Tudor buildings badly in need of a bit of TLC. As for the garden, there was only one rose in it! They got to work – a labour of love over the next twenty years to create what would become one of the most famous gardens on the planet. It's a place that celebrates all that is beautiful, simple and colourful. It's a garden for all seasons, but spring is really special with the snowdrops, daffodils, fritillaries, wood anemones, primroses and tulips all appearing at different times, so there's always something in full bloom.

I am still very French and traditional in some ways, but there's a lot about me that is more British than French. As is probably very clear to you now, I am obsessed with my garden. I wake up thinking about it. Each year, I can't wait for May when the whole place erupts in colour. Just before then, the anticipation is wonderful, knowing that all these flowers are growing underground and they're all going to meet the sun for the first time soon. In fact, I go into my own *Gardeners' World* so much that Fruitcake winds me up about it when I'm in the garden. 'Can I get you a cup of tea, Monty?!' she'll say. Without realising it, I've become the garden equivalent of a 'curtain twitcher' and no one is more surprised than me that I feel this way. I'll peek over my fence like a meerkat checking my neighbours' gardens to see how mine compares. It feels like it's got the most personality and the most love because I spend so much time trying to perfect it. Now, if I were British, I wouldn't dream of saying something so immodest as 'my garden is the best' – I'd just quietly feel it. Luckily, I'm still French, so I can say with confidence that my garden is the best. Did I ever spend any time gardening or even looking at a garden before I moved to the UK? Absolutely not – I couldn't imagine anything more boring. So what on earth explains why I'm at my happiest spending a Sunday afternoon choosing plants in a garden centre?

I love the fact that Brits have a special affinity for each season and making the most of each one. It's reflected in the *Springwatch*, *Winterwatch* and (sadly discontinued) *Autumnwatch* programmes, which I got really into. Maybe the reverence for each season is down to the Celts, who divided up their year with four major festivals: Samhain, Imbolc, Bealtaine and Lughnasa. Incidentally, I took a genealogy test in 2023 and discovered I have Celtic blood, being 6 per cent Welsh, 5 per cent Irish and 5 per cent English. The area around my home town of Limoges was originally a Celtic settlement called Lemovicum, so maybe there's a connection there. Over time, Bealtaine became May Day, and it's still celebrated around the UK. Whitstable, in

Kent, celebrates the Jack in the Green Festival, which involves someone dressing up as 'Jack', with greenery and flowers to symbolise the spirit of spring and the coming of summer.

While we're flying the Kent flag, Canterbury Cathedral is a truly magical place. History, myths and legends are practically seeping out of the walls. I only learned the story of Thomas Becket after I moved to the UK. As I understand it, he was murdered after King Henry II exclaimed in a rage 'Who will rid me of this troublesome priest?!' which four of his knights mistakenly took literally. Death by miscommunication! It made me wonder if the four knights were being very British and didn't want to cause social awkwardness by asking the King to clarify if he was actually ordering them to kill the Archbishop, or if he was just using a figure of speech, like 'I could murder a *pain au chocolat*'. Was committing murder an easier prospect than dealing with an awkward conversation?

Then you've got *The Canterbury Tales*, written by Chaucer in the late fourteenth century, which features a group of pilgrims travelling together from London to Canterbury to visit the shrine of Thomas Becket. I love that the whole idea is a storytelling competition between the pilgrims, with the victor winning a meal (plus drinks) paid for by the others at the Tabard Inn in Southwark. It all feels so wonderfully and timelessly British.

Canterbury Cathedral also has a few French connections. Come to think of it, even the motto of Kent – 'Invicta', meaning 'Unconquered' – has a French connection. It came about because William the Conqueror was forced to take a different route to London because the people of Kent took up arms and tree branches and scared off William's men. The cathedral was destroyed in a massive fire the year after William invaded, and rebuilding began under Lanfranc, the first Norman Archbishop of Canterbury, using stone shipped over from France. Two marriages between the English and French royal families took place in the cathedral in the thirteenth century, including Edward I (later nicknamed 'Longshanks') and Margaret of France. Margaret named their first-born son Thomas after Thomas Becket, whom she'd prayed to during pregnancy. The cathedral is also the resting place of Edward, the Black Prince, who played a big role in the Hundred Years War between England and France. He's not my favourite historical character if I'm honest, seeing as he ransacked my home town of Limoges in 1370. Although, given that

I've got English and Welsh blood, it's quite possible my ancestors were fighting against the French back then!

I fell in love with Southwold in 2020. When you first walk around the quaint streets, soak in the Georgian architecture, wander along the pier with an ice cream, pastel-coloured beach huts in the background, it looks and feels like a quintessential vision of Old England. And then you find out more about it and you realise there are more layers of beauty and texture to the town. In 1659, a fire destroyed most of Southwold. The land on which the buildings stood was never built on again, and it's since become well-kept parkland, which is why the whole town looks like it's peppered with pretty village greens. At the end of the high street, I noticed a plaque to the author George Orwell. He spent much of his youth in Southwold, and came up with his pen name (his real name was Eric Blair) in reference to the River Orwell, which runs through nearby Ipswich. Usually, when you visit a British coastal town, you learn about some beef they've had with the French. But Southwold is a happy rare exception. In 1672, the French and English fleets fought alongside each other just east of Southwold in the Battle of Sole Bay against the Dutch! *Fraternité!*

I had the obligatory fish and chips (you can't not have fish and chips when visiting the British seaside) at the Boardwalk Restaurant on the pier. I love a seaside pier, they are just so British, and Southwold's is one of the best, restored to its former glory. I sat outside with the wind on my face and the salty smell of the sea – perfect. A meditative sense of serenity engulfs me when I'm near water, and I feel at peace. They served up a delicious chunky piece of haddock and perfectly cooked chips – just the right consistency, crispy on the outside and fluffy on the inside – and beautiful mushy peas. I haven't quite yet graduated to vinegar on my chips. Who knows, maybe I will when I've lived here for forty years! All in all, you can't get a much better experience than that. Great food, great service, great view. And a nice mug of tea, too. I like a cup of Earl Grey in the afternoon, with just a splash of milk, so it's the colour of clotted cream fudge. I know that the colour of a cup of tea matters a great deal to Brits. And I know that adding milk to Earl Grey might send me to the ninth circle of Dante's Inferno for some of you, but there you go. Each to their own.

It was amazing to discover that the Southwold Pier, built in 1900, was actually a regular stopping-off point for steamships that travelled from London Bridge, down the Thames and along the coast all the way up to Southwold. It was such a romantic era of travel back then. But all is not lost: there's still a seagoing paddle steamer – the PS *Waverly* – that travels in summer from Great Yarmouth, down to Southwold and Ipswich before docking near Tower Bridge. Who knew?!

I stayed at the Swan, a fantastic hotel with beautifully appointed rooms and perfect service, which always matters a lot to me as you know by now. Best of all, the hotel is right in the centre of town. When I walked out of the front door, I was in the middle of a quaint little market, full of fresh produce, clothes and souvenirs. It felt like I'd travelled back in time. I didn't know about the quirky English tradition of 'kiss-me-quick' hats until I saw the words on a mug and someone explained that this slice of seaside history goes back to Victorian times. I'm more of a 'take your time' kind of guy, though.

There isn't anywhere like Southwold in France. When you look at the French seaside, you're drawn to places like Saint-Tropez, Cannes and Nice, but that's a completely different seaside experience. It's like comparing apples and oranges. Places like Southwold are picturesque, charming and garnished with tradition and history. If you're after those things, as I am, then there's nowhere better. And just when you don't think you can like a place more, you remember that the Adnams brewery and gin distillery is right in the centre of the town. What a place to go for a tour and a cheeky sample of everything they'd give me. You can even make your own gin there. It's the perfect end to a sensory delight of a trip.

One thing I've noticed is that the further you are from London, the more likely people are to say hello or start a chat in the street. This is especially true the further north you go in England. I've found people so friendly in Manchester, which I've got to know well because we filmed series 16–20 of *First Dates* there. It's a completely different vibe to London – people are more open and you end up having these funny chats about nothing at all or getting into these wild conversations. You never know which direction a conversation's going to take and I love it. Also, Mancunian slang is always fun for a foreigner. 'Brew', 'buzzing', 'sound' and 'dead' you can sort of understand. But 'our kid' and especially 'Awright, cock?' took a little explaining the first time. Bearing in mind that Manchester and Liverpool are only thirty miles apart, the difference between a Mancunian accent and a Scouse accent is incredible. Everywhere has its own proud, unique character, flavour and humour. 'All right, my lover?' might be a personal favourite though, from the south-west.

On Friday and Saturday nights, it feels like the whole of Manchester is out and about, and not just young people, having a great time. It's a very sociable city and people are up for a laugh. When I think of Manchester, I think of a party town – happy people in a good mood. I love the place and I love the people. There is something in the water in Manchester, and I'd like a little bit of what they have there down in London.

I went up to the Lake District a few years ago and it was more beautiful than I could have imagined. And for me, the jewel in the crown was Grasmere. It's the perfect spot for a date. There is nothing like a walk in the fells to make you slow down and connect with yourself and the person you love. You can stay in a beautiful pub with amazing food and walk it off in stunning scenery. What more could you want from a holiday, especially in autumn when the leaves are changing colour? I've had a similar experience in Loch Fyne on the Scottish west coast. Oh my God, what a place. You feel like you've been transported into a painting. And then you try the fish and the seafood and you can't help but revel in the fact that Britain has some of the finest food and views on the planet.

Oban, further up the coast, is lovely too. It's such a peaceful seaside town and everywhere you look, you've got dramatic scenery. I visited at the height of summer when the sun sits just beneath the horizon all night and it never gets dark. I knew about the White Nights festivals in Northern Europe where the sun famously doesn't set, but I hadn't experienced one and I had no idea you could catch a little bit of this magic in Britain. I'd never seen a bright night-time sky like that in my life. It was utterly spectacular. I swam in the sea off the coast of Oban and it was as flat as a lake on a windless day. The water's so clear. And then you go and warm yourself up by the fire with a nice dram of whisky. They know how to do things properly up in Scotland.

For *Gordon, Gino and Fred: Road Trip*, we even gave the Highland Games a go. The Highland Games 'heavy events' look like something out of the World's Strongest Man competition. We were surrounded by man mountains, everywhere. Gordon, Gino and I did the Sheaf Toss – tossing a bundle of straw weighing around nine kilos vertically over a bar – and Gordon and I cleared the first bar, though the less said about Gino's effort the better, but he gave it a good stab. What I loved about the Highland Games was that we got to be around the best in the business. I've always loved that feeling that even though you've got no chance of winning, you know that their presence will rub off on you. I want to compete with people who are better than me, whether they're smarter, stronger or faster. I'm a competitive guy and I like to win, but if I lose, I want to know that I've given my best.

I've been to Edinburgh many times, for work but also to go and support my daughter Andrea, because she does a lot of diving competitions up there. Waking up in Edinburgh in the shadow of the castle and walking from the western end of the Royal Mile, you get gloriously lost in intoxicating myths and legends. And then, you walk to the eastern end, by the Scottish Parliament, and five minutes later, you're in the wilderness on the way up to Arthur's Seat. I can't think of any capital city in Europe with a view like that twenty-five minutes from town.

I know that the title of the book is *Seriously British*, but I did want to mention Northern Ireland, because I've been there and had an incredible time. I went to the north coast to stay in a seaside bed and breakfast for *B&B by the Sea* in 2022. The location was spectacular, with Mussenden Temple – built in 1785 and dramatically perched high on a cliff – above the B&B. You can see the Scottish island of Islay just across the water, famous for its incredible peaty whiskies. And talking of whiskeys (don't shoot the editor – that's how they spell it the other side of the Irish Sea), I visited the oldest whiskey distillery in the world on that trip: Bushmills, which traces its history back to 1608. Bushmills is a fantastic place. It's like you're walking around the keep of an old castle. We met with the master blender, Alex Thomas, and she'd been at Bushmills since 2004 and grew up fifteen minutes away from the distillery. Bushmills is an icon of Northern Ireland – so much so, it even appears on their banknotes.

The next day, I encouraged the B&B owners to come with me for a morning sea swim. There was a certain amount of reluctance, given the fact it was early spring and about 7°C. To be fair, it was pretty chilly, but it was so invigorating and there's nothing like it. When you get into the water, you feel like you have to learn how to breathe again. But then you acclimatise and you soak in your surroundings. You emerge from the water and feel so powerful because you realise that you can take it. It reminded me of taking the plunge by getting on that ferry from Calais to Dover aged twenty with my whole life in two suitcases. I'd never felt more alive than I did in Great Britain.

2

'No Sex Please, We're British'

I was eighteen when I had my heart broken for the first time. I was working for the summer season in a restaurant in south-west France. I fell madly in love with a girl who was a chef at the restaurant and we ended up sharing a bedsit for the season. I remember that the lyrics to a song kept ringing through my head because I'd found love – I just had no clue what to do with it.

I'd never experienced such an all-consuming love before. It dominated my waking thoughts and my dreams – it was like there was no escape. So when she told me she *liked me*, I felt like I was about to launch into orbit. And then one evening things were about to start happening between us, and I remember my heart was pounding like a drum 'n' bass track. We kissed and then we were in bed together, naked. But when she gently caressed the back of my leg with her fingers, that was it – my body and my mind couldn't deal with it. Let's just say it was an abrupt end. *No no no!* I couldn't believe it. When she realised what had just happened, she looked at me in horror and shock.

I don't mind sharing this because I know that it's much more common than we think and it's good to look back and laugh at one's embarrassing moments. You combine that heart-surging anticipation, passion, intensity, urges and excitement and there's no way to contain it. The fact that I'd been having sex for two years before that moment provided no protection – sometimes a situation is just too much for you to handle, especially when you're a teenager. So much is going on emotionally. You're only just finding your confidence and self-belief and realising both how you see yourself and maybe how others see you. And then combine that with the pressure you apply on yourself. I told myself afterwards *I'm an adult – aren't I supposed to be able to have sex for hours and hours?!* Apparently not! Thankfully it proved to be a one-off. Otherwise, much like that encounter, this might have been a very short chapter.

I came back home after the season ended. We stayed in touch, as I was still very much in love with her. A month later, she came to stay with me. But just a few days after she left, she called me up and told me it was over. It was out of the blue. I was completely distraught. In almost every single break-up, one person knows what's about to happen and the other is caught by surprise. The one on the receiving end is at their most vulnerable. At the time, I didn't know what to do with myself. I felt such a sense of loss and hopelessness. I didn't know how to feel joy or laugh. Life didn't have any sense of meaning any more. One day, my dad found me sitting on the sofa crying. He reached his arm out and rested my head on his shoulder. 'It's going to be all right, Fred. It's happened to all of us. I know how much it hurts. I know you can't see it now but you're going to be OK. It will pass.' He was right. And now, I use some of the same words to comfort friends, family and First Daters.

In the end, it took me a year to get over her. Two things needed to happen. First, time needed to pass. People say 'Time's a healer' a lot when you're suffering and you never really take it in when you're under siege from your emotions. Time passes so slowly you can hear every echoing tick of the clock. But then one day you start smiling again. You start having fun again, spending more time with your friends and you meet new people. Your perspective changes and you're able to be more objective about the relationship. That's what 'time's a healer' really means. And that's when the second thing happens. You can acknowledge to yourself that that love has passed. You can imagine meeting someone else and feeling that spark again. Then you can turn the page.

To paraphrase French actor Alain Delon, our first love is the purest and most beautiful kind of love because we think it's going to last for ever. And those uniquely powerful feelings linger. Reflecting on it now, I remember how beautiful she was, how much I was in love with her and how heartbroken I was when it ended. It was an opera in three parts. The break-up was awful, but I'm glad I met her.

The stereotype is that Brits are reserved, shy, emotionless and unromantic. It was quite the opposite in the late eighteenth and early nineteenth centuries. Britain was the heart of the Romantic movement, led by poets Keats, Shelley, Byron and Coleridge. The Brits were the great romantics! Everything changed in the Victorian age as the values of self-restraint and stoicism became almost religiously practised. Why this came about is debated, but it could well have something to do with the French! Watching the French Revolution of 1789–1799 from across the English Channel, what started out as the triumph of liberty, equality and brotherhood (*Liberté, Égalité, Fraternité*) deteriorated into violence and chaos. The perception was that the French let their emotions consume them. The Brits feared the same fate. So they buttoned up their blouses and their breeches.

When Britain became the dominant world power, after defeating Napoleon at Waterloo in 1815, the era of the 'stiff upper lip' was on its way. As the Empire expanded, Brits had to present a strong front to their colonial subjects. Displaying emotion was associated with weakness and the Brits couldn't afford to show any cracks. In his 1872 book *The Expression of the Emotions in Man and Animals*, Charles Darwin summed up the sense of British self-control, writing that 'savages weep copiously from very slight causes', whereas 'Englishmen rarely cry, except under the pressure of the acutest grief'. Brits identified themselves with resilience, strength and stoicism. And this persisted for another seventy years, exemplified by the 1940s 'Blitz spirit' and the attitude of 'Keep calm and carry on'. It was only after the war, as the British Empire broke apart, that the cracks in the stiff-upper-lip mentality began to appear. Through the 1960s, the last thing the younger generation wanted to think about was self-control. Suddenly everyone was smoking weed, kissing and making love. What a time to be alive!

My arrival on these shores in the 1990s coincided with another period of profound social change and the era of Britpop and 'Cool Britannia'. Writing this now, I've spent more time living in the UK than I have in France. And while that has its drawbacks – I'm seen as a foreigner in both countries – it does have its advantages. For example, because I'm an outsider, it feels like I can be objective about both my homeland and my adopted home. And I can compare the two in a way that not many people experience. There are some differences that are immediately obvious: you just have to have a conversation with a stranger in France to get the sense that the French are quite exuberant, expansive and extroverted. They wear their hearts on their sleeves. They say what they feel and they feel what they say. This can come as a bit of a shock to Brits, because they are naturally quieter and more reserved than the French. To me, these characteristics are part of the charm of the Brits. I find it sexy, as do a lot of people. With the French, when they're excited about something, it's plain for everyone to see. They literally jump around with emotion. With the Brits, they *feel* the same thing – it's the way they show it that's different. They're shouting and gesturing frantically just like the French are, only it's happening in their heads. Brits jump around on the inside.

And that means when you come to the UK as a foreigner, you don't only need to understand English, you also need to learn another type of language. A language of small gestures and subtle expressions. These delicate arts were lost on me the first time I came to the UK on that two-week student exchange in Stratford-upon-Avon. As a teenage boy, I had other things on my mind. I was here during term time, so I spent the fortnight going to the school that my host family's kids went to. I found myself in assembly with a hundred girls my age wearing long socks and miniskirts. If I'm honest, my first thoughts were something along the lines of 'Holy shit!' and 'Praise the Lord!' Hormones were kicking in big time. My entire life at that point revolved around one thing: kissing girls.

During those two weeks in the UK, I kissed ten girls. That's not an estimate or a figure I've plucked out of the sky for dramatic or comic effect – I remember the number, because I couldn't believe it myself at the time. I still feel that way, looking back on it aged fifty-two. I'm still proud of it!

I hadn't been anywhere near that successful back in France, and I came back home thinking I'd set some kind of Guinness World Record. When I told my friends about it, either they didn't believe me or they started asking their parents to send them on an English exchange.

I remember kissing a girl called Belinda many times. She was very beautiful in a way that I thought of as typically British at the time: blonde hair, blue eyes and a big smile with perfect white teeth. Part of the reason I remember the name was because soon after I got back to France, my mum and dad bought a pet guinea pig. They asked me to think of a good name. Well, there was only one in my head at the time. So I named the family guinea pig Belinda!

As I sat in my room staring at Belinda the guinea pig, I started wondering why I'd done so well on the romantic front in the UK. Was it the French accent? It felt like it had helped. Girls wanted to talk to me and I think my accent was considered quite exotic and exciting. It also helped that my English was good. It was one of my best subjects at school, and it was something that excited me, because it came with the promise of exploring new places around the world. So I applied myself in a studious and serious fashion. And that really paid off on the English exchange because I found that I could communicate properly with everyone. I found the girls very open, curious and sweet in a way I hadn't encountered before in France. They seemed really easy to talk to and that somehow liberated my inner kisser. And something about being in the UK made me feel free and self-confident.

I also realised that I wasn't just in love with kissing British girls – I was also in love with Britain. I loved the excitement in the school playground, the banter going on before the teacher turned up, the informal school lunches, the more relaxed rules and the general sense of fun. That helped make it so easy to talk to people. I went back to France after the English exchange full of confidence and hoping that I'd be able to emulate my success back home. But it just didn't happen. My powers only worked in Britain! So I was desperate to return. Britain had become the promised land across the water.

In the end, I didn't return to the UK for several years, but the next time I did, with those two suitcases, it was *for good*. During those intervening years, I experienced a fairly typical adolescence in France. When I share my memories of that time with my British friends, the one thing that always surprises them is when I say that we grow up in France talking about sex. Just saying the word 'sex' can make a Brit blush. Even inside their heads, Brits go red and get all flustered. But what I've learned is that while many Brits might not be comfortable talking about sex, they're thinking about it just as much as everyone else!

British friends tell me that there's nothing more awkward than the conversation parents initiate with their children around the age of sixteen about sex. Apparently, everyone gets flustered, coughs a lot and can't wait to leave the room. It's very different in France. We are surrounded by sex – in films, in adverts, in music. When I turned sixteen, my mum bought me a pack of condoms. 'Fred, you're sixteen years old now, you need to be responsible and take precautions,' she told me. It was all very matter-of-fact and not weird in the least.

Having this kind of conversation is very much in keeping with the way we grow up. For example, nudity is perfectly normal. I saw my parents naked all the time when I was a boy. We were all naked. No one was self-conscious. A lot of my friends in the UK have told me that they've never seen their parents naked. That surprised me the first time I heard it.

Anyway, by the time I turned sixteen, pretty much everyone in my year at school had been talking about sex for a while. If you fancied someone, you told them. You communicated how you felt because you wanted something to happen. When I learned about what people experienced here, with boys in one corner whispering and laughing about fancying someone and the girls giggling in another corner, I wondered how anyone actually ends up having sex at all!

If you talk about something enough, it just becomes something completely normal. And if you either avoid the subject or discuss it secretly, it's easy to see how sex and nakedness can become taboo subjects. I think this is why a lot of Brits respond to conversations about sex by wincing, going red, getting all worked up inside their heads and saying things like 'Oh God', 'Oh wow' and 'Oh my'. This has always fascinated me because it's almost like a reflex reaction – you don't know you're doing it! It's the one time that Brits can't *keep calm and carry on*.

Dr Jacques Waynberg, the famous French sexologist, said: 'The problem is that the British take sex too seriously, too ponderously, as something deeply personal and secret, to be hidden and discussed in whispers, or conversely, something smutty to be gossiped about.'

Whenever I quote that to a Brit, they often laugh. The kind of uniquely British humble and restrained laugh of acknowledgement that indicates you might be on to something. One British friend of mine offered up a slightly different insight. 'Or we just deal with the subject by not dealing with it.' In France, we tend to confront things head-on. And while I'm not saying this is always the right way, it does often help. When I was growing up, sixteen-year-old girls and boys were talking freely – together – about sex. And most of them were having sex. It wasn't a big deal. Everyone knew the places people went to have sex, like the embankment of the river Dordogne, which ran through Souillac, where I went to catering college. Parties in my late-teenage years involved having sex upstairs and taking a break to dance downstairs. We were like rampant rabbits.

I remember having long conversations with friends about love, sex and relationships. They were just part of growing up to us, evolving naturally and normally. The conversation is still evolving as I'm progressing through life. It's part of who I am. And so, for example, when I'm working on *First*

Dates, and people say something sweet like: 'Fred, you're a modern-day Cupid – you talk about love so naturally,' the truth is that I've been doing this since I was that sixteen-year-old kid. It's completely natural to me and part of everyday life.

My first foray into fixing a relationship was aged ten. My brother Pierre was seven and he had a problem. He was in love. But, alas, Catherine was already going out with this guy called David, as much as you can 'go out' with someone when you're seven years old. But undaunted, Pierre announces his love for her and tells her how much he wants to be with her, down on one knee and all that. She answers: 'Pierre, I am with David but I will love you if you bring me a piece of the moon.' Pierre comes back home and tells me this, absolutely distraught. He doesn't know what to do! So I had a think and said to him, 'Don't worry about it, Pierre. Go to the neighbour, Madame Picat, and get her to give you some coffee grains.' Madame Picat had one of those fancy coffee machines and I had a plan. We'd paint the coffee grains white, and it would pass for moon rock. Then Pierre would present it to Katrin and tell her that there was no distance he wouldn't travel for her love. As it turns out, she actually loved him more than David and wanted to be with him but also wanted to make him work for it. She appreciated the gesture, though.

I've always been fascinated by people and how they work. I want to understand and help them, and if I can call on my own experience to do that, I will. I'm not providing anything extraordinary or new – I just go straight to the point and ask direct questions about what people want and what they like. It's about them and only them. I know that some people watching *First Dates* will be thinking 'Oh my God – what are you saying?!' but they're important things to raise. I know how useful it is to bring these questions up openly and honestly because the answers are going to help them. Some people need encouragement to be free and comfortable to express and communicate how they feel. And this is maybe where it helps to talk to someone who isn't British, because I don't have to play by the rules. I can cut to the chase. When I notice that a Brit has gone red about something I've asked or said, I might mention that they seem embarrassed so that I can try to understand more about what's going on. If they're honest enough to recognise their embarrassment openly and laugh about it, which often happens, then I take it as a sign that they're OK to continue that conversation. That's how I approach British shyness.

Maybe this is one of the reasons why *Fifty Shades of Grey* was such a smash hit, because it brought something 'naughty' into the mainstream. It was full-on rather than discreet and private. Inside their heads, of course, Brits love sex. All that 'no sex please, we're British' stuff is rubbish. They love thinking about sex, but talking about it openly and feeling comfortable with it is another matter.

Inside British heads, I feel like there's an imaginary line, a kind of barrier that prevents you from disclosing too much too soon. If two Brits are both behind their own barriers, then the conversation will just be small talk. It'll be friendly, cover 'neutral' topics and you can share a little laugh without anything getting meaningful. But all you need is the right combination of words or the right environment, and everything changes. For example, after a couple of pints in the pub, everyone happily crosses the barrier together. Or if you're in an unfamiliar place where convention goes out the window, like the waiting room of an accident and emergency department or when you're on holiday, there's no line any more. Anything goes!

Sometimes I have a bit of fun with British shyness. I am who I am, I do what I do and I say what I say. And as such, I know that sometimes I can shock a Brit with something that sounds perfectly normal to me. To be honest, I can be a little cheeky, even with a French audience. My mum nicknamed me *le provocateur* when I was growing up because I like to push the envelope. She still calls me that. It's something of a French cultural tradition to push the envelope, and I was inspired by Serge Gainsbourg, the greatest *provocateur* of them all. He spent a lifetime testing boundaries. His legendary duet with Jane Birkin, '*Je t'aime … moi non plus*', in 1969, with its sexual lyrics (and noises) were too much for some countries, who banned it. The UK didn't though, and it became the first foreign-language song to reach number one in the UK charts. And while Serge did achieve international fame for a while, the cultural impact he had in France was both immense and long-lasting. He helped change our perspective of normal in romantic and sexual terms. Suddenly, average became mundane. Culturally, maybe he made all of us a bit more provocative.

I like to get a reaction from Brits sometimes because I know the buttons to press. As long as it's done in a playful, kind spirit rather than with the intention to make someone feel bad, embarrass them or offend them, then it's just a bit of fun. And it runs both ways – you have to be able to give and receive. I believe that's how you gain respect and appreciation for each other.

I've grown up comfortable in my skin, and, if anything, that's actually improved with age. How does that manifest itself? I sometimes just take my clothes off. It happens a lot at home or when I'm with Gino and we want to wind Gordon up. It's so easy to wind him up, it's practically a hobby. Instantaneous nudity does shock Gordon. But to be fair, instantaneous nudity shocks a lot of Brits. Even Speedos seem to shock a lot of Brits! I wear them because I love swimming and you can't swim fast wearing swimming shorts. I've always worn them. But when I go to the pool with my Speedos, I can see people – both men and women – thinking 'Oh my God – he's wearing Speedos!' The same thing happens on social media as soon as I post a picture of me wearing them. Some people are shocked. They're stunned that I'm not shy or embarrassed. I'm confident, have a good relationship with my body and the outside world, and I'm not concerned with how other people look at me. So I've no reason to be embarrassed. I'm just going for a swim in my Speedos – I'm not shooting a porn film!

I think a lot of shyness and reserve is about not feeling comfortable in your own skin. And much of that comes from comparing yourself to other people. I wonder why we can't be more in tune with our emotions and accept who we are. If we're not, it makes life an unsettling experience, doesn't it? And that might reveal itself as embarrassment or feeling out of place when there's nothing to feel ashamed about. I'm confident and comfortable with myself but I'm not immune to embarrassment. I was frightened about going on the *Strictly Come Dancing* Christmas Special in 2021. I was scared of not being able to dance and petrified of making a fool of myself, especially because I knew my kids would be watching. But I've learned that delivering something that you didn't know you could do is what gives you confidence. The more you put yourself out there, the better you feel. So I said yes when the producers of the show invited me to come on precisely because I was scared. I took it as a sign for me to rise to the challenge.

Maybe I need to encourage British people to loosen up a little, which will allow them to be more able to talk about sex without blushing. When more and more people talk about something, it becomes normal. It's no longer shocking and just becomes part of everyday life. So if, for example, more Brits are talking openly about sex, the embarrassment factor will diminish. And that means fewer of my British friends will go red and get all flustered as soon as I ask something about sex!

To be fair, attitudes towards sex and romance are changing in the UK. Sexuality is evolving, and the Brits are on it. Open relationships and polyamory are becoming more mainstream now. In the past, they weren't even things that people would discuss. Now they're all over the papers, on social media and on television.

Just look at the number and variety of dating shows there are on TV. Back in the 1980s, there was just one dating show – *Blind Date* – but you could sense how much of an appetite there was given that over 18 million people tuned in to watch Cilla Black every week. Now, you've got *First Dates*, *Love Island*, *Geordie Shore*, *I Kissed a Boy*, *I Kissed a Girl* and *Naked Attraction* among many others. Some of them are very good, some are not as good, some are very funny – they all have a different angle. But anyone claiming that the Brits are *too* reserved just needs to watch five minutes of *Naked Attraction* or *Geordie Shore*.

There are still taboos, of course, and things people don't want to discuss or admit to, but it all still happens. Former British boxer David Haye is public about his three-way relationship on Instagram. People are having whatever kind of relationship they like regardless of whether other people are condoning or condemning it. I think we need to have an open mind about what goes on behind closed doors. I see David Haye's photos on Instagram and I think 'It's good if you can get it!' – to use one of my favourite British expressions, which in classic British fashion manages to combine admiration, self-deprecation and a teaspoon of playful envy.

Attitudes towards both kissing and going to bed with someone on the first date are changing too. My feelings are: if you're both happy about it, why wait? What is the rule you're breaking? Why it's acceptable for a man to sleep with somebody on the first date but not for a woman is beyond me. Thankfully, it seems to be becoming more equal. Women are increasingly asserting what they want and how they want it and they're doing things their way.

I think one of the reasons *First Dates* is so successful is that Brits, who are, generally speaking, naturally quite shy, find it liberating to see real dates and hear dating, romance and sex talked about quite openly. It feels like a cultural evolution is happening before our eyes. And I've witnessed this in the time I've been doing the show. You only have to go back to the first couple of series compared to now and you can see how much the dial has changed. Brits are getting less and less shy and that's going to continue. I'm not saying that there's going to be such a dramatic shift that Brits will be as candid as the French, but I wouldn't want them to be anyway. I love how differently the Brits and the French take joy in things. The points of difference between us are constant sources of wonder, amusement and surprise to each other.

The way both countries treat high-profile affairs fascinates me. In the UK, it's a national scandal and all the details are laid bare in the newspapers. In France, it's more like 'Oh, someone's having an affair, are they? What's for lunch?' François Hollande, the French president from 2012 to 2017, was caught by a photographer driving from the Élysée Palace (the president's official residence) to his mistress's apartment on a moped, but you have to wonder how many times he'd been making that trip without anyone seeing him. Apparently one of his security detail used to turn up in the morning to deliver croissants. François Mitterand (president from 1981 to 1995) managed to have a secret second family with Anne Pingeot, the curator of sculpture at the Louvre. They called their daughter Mazarine, named after the oldest public library in France, which faces the Louvre, across the River Seine. Apparently, Anne was keen on that name because it was so unusual that it wouldn't be chosen by any of Mitterand's other mistresses!

I think Brits are inwardly very romantic. They understand love as much as anyone. It wasn't a Frenchman or an Italian who wrote *Romeo and Juliet*, the greatest love story of all time – it was William Shakespeare. I developed a fascination for Shakespeare after I came to the UK. Maybe that was something to do with the fact that that exchange when I kissed all the girls was in Stratford-upon-Avon, his birthplace. I think it's significant that Shakespeare was British (or *English*, I should say, given that this was before the Treaty of Union). And maybe it's the reason why his life is shrouded in so much mystery. It could be that he just liked observing people from afar while quietly and studiously keeping himself to himself, away from the drama. Underneath the beautiful rhymes, Shakespeare encapsulates what it is to be human. That's why the trials and tribulations he wrote about are still relevant today. We all experience love, romance, friendship, jealousy, envy, temptation and betrayal, and he captures the raw, intense essence of these emotions. He understood how people function and he had an ability to analyse people and say things as they were. He could provide exquisite, memorable and inspirational words of wisdom. And that's why I think Shakespeare would have been the ultimate maître d' for the *First Dates* restaurant! He could turn thoughts into action, and sometimes that's what Brits need a bit of help with.

I remember seeing a survey a few years ago that listed the top romantic gestures according to British men. Numbers 1 and 2 were a surprise bouquet of flowers and cooking dinner. *So far so good, gents*, I thought! Then things took a nosedive. 'Taking the bins out' and 'Putting the toilet seat down' were numbers 5 and 7. They're gestures, sure, but they're not exactly going to get anyone's pants off. Being romantic is about the sweet little gestures. It's about remembering the early days of courtship when the only thing you can think about is the other person. So maybe you send an impromptu text in the middle of the day or you surprise them outside work. A tender Post-it note on the kettle or taking time out to go for a walk together can be so romantic – it doesn't have to be an expensive gift, everyone's got different means. It's about showing how much you think of them and how much they're present inside your head. Or you can plan something special in advance for Valentine's Day.

I like to celebrate Valentine's Day because it's the day of love. It's a day that is just about you and your partner. The surprise, the anticipation and the knowledge that someone is thinking about you makes it exciting. It's also an opportunity to be playful. This year, I was abroad for Valentine's Day, but when I unpacked my suitcase in my hotel room, I found a beautiful Valentine's card from Fruitcake. The gesture and the words really touched my heart. I had also left a surprise for her, but had taken a slightly different approach: a small full-length Greek statue wearing a pair of red Speedos. 'It looks just like you,' she said when we WhatsApped that evening, taking off the Speedos. 'It's lifesize!'

I've seen a unique side of Valentine's Day in the UK, having been a maître d' for as long as I have. First of all, every restaurant is booked. You could sell every table ten times over. Everyone wants to go somewhere fancy. In the restaurant, it's just tables for two so the whole layout looks different. And the atmosphere is much more charged, so that feels different too. There are three types of table. The first type (the majority) is very sweet, laughing and enjoying each other's company. Then you've got the second type: the couples who have very little or nothing to say to each other. That's not to say that they're not having a good time, though – they might be. And then you've got the third type. The couple who suddenly start having an argument. It's easy to see why this happens. Maybe they don't go out very much, for whatever reason, so there might be added stress about an occasion where there's already a certain amount of pressure, and something blows. There's nothing the couple can do about it – it's beyond their control and the couple is almost as surprised as everyone else. I think it can actually be a good thing. Sometimes you have to burst the abscess for a wound to heal. There will probably be at least three arguments in a restaurant on Valentine's night. So, as a maître d', you have to be on your game. You need to be careful about when to approach a table and when to give people privacy; you have to be sensitive, discreet and alive to your surroundings. It's prepared me well for the *First Dates* restaurant.

On *First Dates*, I spend a lot of time just observing people in the restaurant. I try to read their body language and expressions, which can often reveal far more than someone is telling you. I watch what they say and how they say it. All this allows me to get a sense of who they are and what they want in a partner. And once I've got a sense of all that, I head straight for the truth, as usual. I ask things like, *What is it you're looking for? What is it you want? What are you hoping for today? What do you think might be getting in the way? Why now?* I care about everyone who appears in front of me on the show and every question I ask is because I want to help them and support them. Sometimes that involves asking them questions they might not have asked themselves, in the hope that it will help them understand themselves a little better, or see the situation in a clearer light. It's all about them.

The *First Dates* job is a perfect extension of what I've been doing for my whole career. And in a way, it's simpler. When I'm the maître d' of a restaurant, people come to dinner for many different reasons: birthdays, engagements, graduations, catching up with old friends. On *First Dates*, they're there for one reason: to meet the love of their life. For some people, *First Dates* is a kind of last-chance love saloon and these daters need a helping hand. And they trust us to deliver. This is why I feel an enormous sense of responsibility for what I do and I take it very seriously.

Part of the reason the series has been going on for so long is because our reputation is good. People trust us. We want them to feel like they are in the right hands. We want them to know that we are going to do our best to make sure their trust is rewarded. Sure, we have fun, but we're not there to make fun of people. We're there to provide an experience and to make sure we create memories for everyone. And that extends beyond the guests. I'm the public face of the restaurant but I'm a single cog in a machine. The work that goes in before I've even said 'Hello' to anyone is immense. The production team sift through the thousands of applications we receive. Then we've got to select the right daters. That involves building a half-inch-thick dossier for each couple explaining the reasons why two people could be a good match. And that can only take you so far, because there's no substitute for chemistry. But we do everything we can that's within our power. We make sure we choose the right venue. It has to be well run, spacious and uplifting. We've got to get the menu right. And then, the daters see me – the last line of defence, or the first line of defence, depending on which way you want to see it.

In our latest series of *First Dates*, filmed in Bath, I'm really proud that we've had the most 'yeses' to the question 'Would you like to see other again?' It might also be the series that has connected with me most personally, because for the first time on *First Dates*, I've brought friends of mine onto the show as daters. I'm practising what I'm preaching! I'm thrilled that *First Dates* can be the beginning of something beautiful for a couple. While you never know how a date is going to go, everyone's there for the same reason really. Underneath we're all the same. We all have the same basic needs: we want warmth, we want love, we want respect, we all want to be trusted, we all want companionship and we want to create memories.

I think a big part of the success of this latest series is down to the city itself. Bath is an incredibly romantic place, with its beautiful honey-coloured Georgian stone, its Roman history, river, gardens and greenery. The dim street lighting at night and the fact that much of the city is pedestrianised means it's the perfect place for a moonlit wander. You feel like you're in a charming village in the middle of Somerset in the eighteenth century. The streets have got these poetic names, like Quiet Street, Bridewell Lane, Plumtree Street and Hay Hill. Even the street signs are beautiful, carved directly into the old stone. The whole place feels like a romance novel has come to life.

The restaurant is in a 250-year-old building. It's almost like a theatre or a place of worship with its rotunda bar, gallery, domed ceiling, Corinthian pillars, intricate plasterwork and beautiful symmetry. It's light, bright and full of life. It gives all the cast and crew a good feeling even before the cameras have started rolling. And when you put all those things together, it's no wonder it creates such a positive impression in the minds of the daters when they walk in. It's such a romantic place. And that's likely to influence and inform the next feeling they have, which is often optimistic and relaxed. It has a magical effect. Then they meet me, and I'm smiling and really pleased to welcome them. The principle is simple. You've got to see, smile and say hello to people before they see, smile and say hello to you. I believe it's my job to be charming first, both in a restaurant and when I'm in love! I want to give generously and from the heart. That's the spirit of hospitality and of love. People will want to give you what they've received. If they see smiley, twinkly eyes, they're more likely to return the gesture. Everyone wants to feel warmth and to feel attractive. I love being able to put them at ease. I love meeting people and striking up a conversation. You never know what you're going to discover.

I believe that if you're amenable to finding good things, you will. And that works the other way around too. If you go somewhere expecting it to be a bad experience, it can cause a negative domino effect where everything feels like it's going wrong. So if you start with a negative first impression, you're setting yourself up to fail because a miracle is going to have to occur to transform your thinking. But if we set up everything to give daters a good first impression, that means they're going to be smiling. And what better way to greet the future love of your life? I met Fruitcake heading down the road in Peckham. I looked up at a beautiful girl who was just about to walk past and she was looking at me, smiling. It was such an attractive smile and there was so much depth to it. Even her eyes were smiling. They were shining and so full of life and energy. There was a joy, warmth, kindness and curiosity and I got that from her before we'd even said a word to each other. I was completely lost inside her eyes and I just said 'Hi!' without even thinking. She said 'Hi!' and we began chatting. I said 'Shall we go for a drink?' and she said 'Yeah! When?' 'Let's go tonight!' I said. She said 'OK!' and we exchanged numbers.

We'd fallen in love and organised our first date within five minutes.

She gave me a call in the afternoon, we met in the evening and that was that. It was a wonderful night. Powerful. Effortless. Beautiful. I'll always remember it. It was all so easy, so simple. It was exactly what I'd been looking for and everything I wanted. Incredibly, we were both thinking of the same famous quote at the same time (only we found that out later): 'When I saw you I fell in love, and you smiled because you knew.'

3

'They're Too Meek and Mild'

The French think that the British don't like making a fuss. That they'd rather put up with something than complain about it. And let me tell you, the French know a thing or two about complaining. If there was an Olympic event in complaining, the French would take the gold. And they'd wear that medal with pride. Complaining is a national pastime. We've even got several words for 'complain'. '*Se plaindre*' is used to complain to someone about something that isn't up to scratch. But then we crank it up a notch with '*porter plainte*', which is when you're lodging an official complaint. And there's also the more light-hearted '*râler*', which is our constant state of moaning and groaning. It's perfectly normal to start a conversation with a complaint. My dad won't mind me saying that he often does. 'The country's going to pot,' he'll say. He's been saying that for forty years. As have millions of people all around France. And they secretly love it. If we entered a period of unrivalled prosperity, topped the medal table at the Olympics and were declared the 'happiest place to live on the planet', we'd still find something to complain about. It's in our blood. 'The French complain of everything, and always' is a famous historical quote about the French mindset. You'd be forgiven for imagining it was a Brit or a German who said that. Henry VIII perhaps? Lord Nelson maybe? Bismarck possibly? It was Napoleon Bonaparte.

The British can get quite worked up about complaining. They feel like they'll cause a scene or upset someone. That means Brits often choose to put up with something they're not happy with. When faced with the question at the hairdresser or barber, 'Are you happy with your haircut?' after a mirror has been held up to the back of their head, I'm not sure any Brit in history has ever responded with 'No'. I do, all the time. If it's not right, I'll tell the barber. I don't want to look like a muppet when I come out! But Brits will prioritise the feelings of someone else (someone who they don't even know) over themselves. It's lovely but it stops you from getting what you actually want. It's not your fault that something isn't right!

So when did the French develop a reputation for complaining? I've never found a definitive answer but I wonder if it's down to the French Revolution. When you come up with a motto as good as '*Liberté, Égalité, Fraternité*' maybe you're destined to fail. Perhaps we set the bar too high and we were always going to fall short. And maybe that's why complaining has entered the national consciousness, because we're constantly comparing the current situation with an unreachable ideal.

During the revolution, the French took to the streets to create what they thought was going to be a better world. It taught us that the people have the power to change things. That attitude hasn't changed in nearly 250 years. We are brought up on strikes in France. It's part of our DNA. Sometimes that leads to farcical situations where people joining a strike have no idea what the strike is about. I remember watching an interview about the latest pension strike and why people had joined the demonstration. Everyone the interviewer spoke to gave a different answer and they had different demands. That wasn't a surprise to me. I've organised strikes myself and can't even remember now what we were actually striking about. But at the time something didn't seem right and we felt duty-bound to change it, so we took to the streets. I remember ringing up my mum (a former nurse) a few years ago and it sounded quite noisy in the background. 'Where are you?' I asked. 'We're demonstrating, Fred.' 'What are you demonstrating for?' 'For the patients and our rights. We've just taken a break to have lunch at a restaurant that does a "*menu ouvrier*" [workers' lunch] – fifteen euros for three courses with half a bottle of wine and coffee!' They've been doing this kind of thing for as long as I can remember. It's like a day out!

It's very different in Britain. The French protest at the drop of a *chapeau* but it takes something big for the Brits to take to the streets. And when they do, they'll bring their inimitable self-knowledge and sense of humour with them. Some of the banners that people created for the anti-Brexit marches in 2019 were just incredible, and they were very revealing about the mentality of the British. 'This doesn't seem very well thought through', 'I'm British and I'm on a march – things must be BAD!', 'Stop being silly' and 'I'm really not happy about any of this'. It's all part of the culture of politeness, being considerate and not really wanting to shake things up, even when they're on a march. Brits want to make sure that everyone's happy and no one feels uncomfortable. One of the funniest examples of this is Brits saying sorry when someone bumps into them. British social anthropologist Kate Fox carried out an experiment for her 2004 book *Watching the English* where she'd deliberately bump into Brits across towns and cities in the UK. Around 80 per cent of 'victims' apologised to her.

Just before the revolution, France was bankrupt. The country was waging an expensive war in America and Louis XVI liked to spend a lot of money. The state was poorly managed, the King was weak, uninterested and badly advised (or he chose his advisers badly) and kept making mistakes. At that point in time, the nobility and the clergy who were at the very top of society were extremely small in number. Underneath that was the rapidly growing bourgeoisie, and then the working class, who comprised around 90 per cent of the population. The group that was influential and instrumental in fomenting the revolution was the bourgeoisie. They were aided by the working class, who were taken along for the ride. The members of the nobility were all executed or exiled, and it must have seemed that the immortal words of the revolution were coming true. A classless society of freedom, equality and brotherhood. The perception from outside France to this day is that we still have a classless society, but it's not true now and it certainly wasn't true then. The existing social hierarchy was replaced with a new structure, just one with lines that weren't as clearly defined as they had been before.

Like the UK, we do have the elite, the middle class and the working class, but we do things differently.

Unlike almost every other subject I can think of, when it comes to talking about class, the Brits are more open than the French. That's not because they want to avoid talking about it; it's because class is hidden within the construct and fabric of society. The other thing that's hidden is wealth itself. In France, we're uncomfortable showing what we call '*signes extérieurs de richesse*' – outward displays of wealth. And that's because it goes against the essence of '*Liberté, Égalité, Fraternité*'. Those words are the *raison d'être* of France, so you don't want to be seen to contradict them. It's different in Britain – wealth and success are celebrated. But like the Brits, the French enjoy the good life. They just have to conceal it. The amount of money in the two countries is remarkably similar. The GDP is almost identical, as is the number of millionaires. And in terms of concentration of wealth, in both countries, 1 per cent of the population owns 23 per cent of the wealth, according to Ipsos' 'Perils of Perception' study in 2017. But past events have affected their ability to display it in public. In France, the cultural impact of the revolution is still very much alive.

In the UK, Brits celebrate the monarchy, and the high-profile events – the coronations, the jubilees, the State Opening of Parliament, the state funerals, the royal weddings – all feature incredible displays of wealth, from carriages to Crown jewels. I watched Harry and Meghan's wedding at my boxing gym in Herne Hill with my friend Clinton. We were both transfixed. It was so over the top, like an incredible fairy tale come to life. In France, you would never see anything like that. When Emmanuel Macron was elected president in 2017, he chose to walk by himself across the courtyard of the Palais du Louvre to a lone lectern. It was slow, solemn and symbolic, and he made sure he got *Liberté, Égalité, Fraternité* into the speech. The words of the revolution are always there, in everything we do.

It must seem bizarre to Brits that someone who is absolutely at the top of the social spectrum, like Macron, can call upon the words of the revolution, which overthrew the elite. While he can't flaunt his status and wealth, his privileged status comes across in other ways. The way he speaks, for example – the words he chooses, his turn of phrase, his refined and precise diction, the way he articulates himself – is beautiful to behold. Macron has mastered French. Of course, that's not how everyone feels. Some people perceive his confidence and intelligence to be pretentious and feel like he acts as if he is better and smarter than everybody else. The way we speak French depends on our class. If you're working class, your French is more rugged, more street. It won't be as subtle or as elegant. Macron's at one end of the scale, but it always seems to surprise Brits to learn that I'm down the other end. I'm as working class as they come.

Both my parents were nurses in the local hospital. We lived in a nice house close to the hospital, but as my brother Pierre has pointed out, it's actually a lot like a British housing estate, where most people rent their homes, though some eventually buy them from their landlords. Limoges was where the CGT (the General Confederation of Labour) was established in 1895, after a dispute in a shoe factory. It became the first of the five great French trade unions. Before we moved there, we lived in a block of flats. Part of the reason my parents chose that house was because they didn't want to worry about petrol costs to commute to work. This was the 1980s when oil prices were soaring and some people working in the hospital couldn't afford the petrol to drive there. My parents didn't want that to happen to them.

My parents taught me about being kind, honest, hard-working, reliable, loyal, trustworthy and being good at what you do. These are all really important values to them. Being nurses, they weren't earning a fortune. My dad did night shifts to make more money and he thought he was very well paid, especially compared to my mum. My dad's friends were all working class, though he had one friend who had his own company and lived in a bigger house than us. I remember going to that house and being surprised that there was a big pond in the garden where you could fish. He and his wife drank much more expensive wine than my parents ordinarily drank. Their kids were much posher than me. There were two different types of kid at school. The ones who could buy *pains au chocolat* and the ones who couldn't. I couldn't. Likewise, the kids who bought the *pains au chocolat* wore branded clothing. There was a brand that all the cool kids wore – Chevignon, which was founded in the late 1970s and became really popular in the 1980s. My parents couldn't afford such things.

In our family, only my auntie and uncle were on a slightly higher social level. Or at least that was how we perceived it. They were both teachers, earned more and spent time with similar people. Their interests were also more intellectual. Whereas my dad would play boules in his spare time, my uncle collected stones. The money my parents did have they spent on food. Really great food, like fillet steak and fresh Dover sole. We went on holiday twice a year, skiing in February and to the seaside in the summer. They focused on the basics. Eat well, have a roof over our heads and have fun on holiday. I'm happy to be labelled as working class. I don't find it derogatory or negative. I know where I come from and I'm proud of it. *C'est tout.* My parents didn't have particularly happy childhoods, and their main aim was to give us what they hadn't had. As a parent, I judge myself by my parents' standards, so, at the least, I endeavour to give my children what my parents gave me. It can be more, but it can't be less. That's the foundation that has guided my life.

At the catering college I went to in Souillac, most of the kids were working class. Only a handful had more means, with pocket money from their parents to get them whatever they needed or wanted. I had enough to get me a few croissants spread out during the week, but if I wanted anything like clothes or shoes, I worked in restaurants at the weekends for cash in hand. I've been working ever since.

One of the kids I met at catering college was a guy who I really liked. He was one of the few from the higher echelons of society – his dad had a very well-paid job and they lived in a big flat in central

Toulouse. I went there once and had dinner with my friend and his family. After we'd finished, I started clearing the plates, and the mum said to me, 'Oh, don't worry, Fred – the maid will do it tomorrow.' That moment stayed with me because I was faced with how the other half live, as Brits would say. But it didn't stop us from becoming friends. Back at home I told my parents about it and mentioned that I'd invited him to come and stay with us. My dad looked at me and said, 'He's never going to come here.' I was quite upset by that. So I said: 'Why do you say that? Because we're a different class? You'll see – he'll come.' But my dad was right – my friend never came. It was a moment where I realised that when you're on different rungs of the social ladder, you won't be on an equal footing. And it still resonates with me.

My mum was really upset that I wanted to go to catering college because she knew it was going to be tough and that I'd be working when other people were on holiday, but she also didn't consider it to be aspirational. She thought university was *the* path towards the higher echelons of society. That's what my super-bright brother Pierre did – and got a PhD. I knew how some members of my family felt about my choice when I went with my parents to a dinner party at my elderly aunt's house about a year or two after I'd started catering college, and my aunt said, '*Ah, le garçon de café*,' in a derogatory, mocking way. I've always remembered that. But for my parents, this period of time was probably quite traumatic, because not only did their elder son want to be a waiter and then move to the UK, but even their younger son, who followed the kind of path they wanted, moved to the UK a few years later. It must have been a difficult adjustment.

Working in hospitality at nice restaurants means that you meet some very interesting and very wealthy customers – rock stars, footballers, CEOs, aristocrats, landowners. But that can lead to a problem: sometimes, because they've been moving in that world, people in hospitality can confuse themselves with the people they're looking after. It is easy to see how it happens – and I've seen it happen many times – but you need to stay grounded. You're looking after them but not sitting at their table. You're not jumping in a Rolls-Royce with a chauffeur after service to go back home. I'll never be that. I haven't gained a false impression of who I am and where I've come from just because I've been on television over the past ten years. I know people recognise me now but I'm not in the same category as those people. For me, it's important to have a house, good food on the table and education for my children. I want to make sure that we're stable for the long term. That's more important to me than being flashy to people who don't know me. I don't have any desire to impress people. At home, I'm a shorts and T-shirt kind of guy!

I found out very quickly working in hospitality in the UK that Brits tend not to be that direct. You learn to read between the lines, which means paying particular attention to not only their words, but also their tone, facial expressions, gestures and body language. You learn to deduce what they might not be telling you as well as what they are. This is all vital because you've got to understand your customers in order to deliver the best service you can, so that they'll come back again and also tell their friends and family about how good it was. It's not enough to hear an 'It was all right' from a customer, because that's not going to get you another booking. So if I know or suspect the customer isn't 100 per cent happy, I'll ask: 'Are you sure there isn't anything that we could have done better?' so we can fix it, especially because that customer might not be the only one feeling that way. As you know, if I don't understand something, I'll say so, straight away. When I first arrived in the UK, I was asking questions all the time. If a customer used a British expression I didn't quite follow, like 'The bread's seen better days' or 'The chef's had a blinder', I'd ask them to explain it for me. Brits don't realise quite how beautifully varied the English language is when it comes to describing how something looks or tastes or how they feel.

As I've said earlier, in hospitality you have to find a way to connect with everyone, which is what I do on *First Dates*. That's the name of the game. If you don't, people will go somewhere else. It's not just about the food, the decor or the ambience of a restaurant. It's about how the front-of-house people make the customers feel. That's the art of hospitality: making people feel welcome and like they've come to the right place. Yes, different nationalities express themselves in different ways and a city like London can be a challenge when customers in a restaurant might be a melting pot of cultures and countries. But, universally, we all have the same basic human needs. If you start from that basis, you can't get it wrong. You need to engage and connect with people on a human level. Everybody reacts to kindness, generosity and humour. You just have to know how to apply it and in what doses.

The Brits and the French are very different in restaurants. If you imagine two restaurants, one full of French people and one full of Brits, and you served bread that was a bit stale, you'd get two very different responses. In the restaurant with French people, on pretty much every table, someone would say 'This bread is hard' or, if they're really unhappy, 'This bread is disgusting'. So you need to have an appropriate answer for them and seize the opportunity to fix the situation. You know what they like and you know what it'll take to win them over. The French aren't going to fake a smile and won't shut up if they're still unhappy.

In the restaurant full of Brits, they'd just eat the bread.

Brits will most likely internalise their unhappiness, but it doesn't mean they feel any different. They're just as unhappy as the French – they just don't tell you. So you've got to find a way to connect your brain to their brain so you can detect anything that's wrong or they're not happy with. Maybe they're avoiding eye contact or they've made a slight wince and you need to be perceptive to read it. You've got to be constantly on the lookout for your guests but you have to do it discreetly so you don't look like you're spying on them. When you've been working in hospitality for long enough, you don't even notice you're doing it. It becomes second nature. And then you've got to ask the right questions. 'Is everything all right? Are you enjoying the bread? Are you sure?' you might ask. Working in the UK, you learn to adapt to the fact that your clientele is quieter, more reserved and less vocal than some other nationalities, and you have to pay attention to little details. I haven't just been doing this during my working life. I've been doing this since I was a boy, and it comes straight from my parents.

I remember one morning when I was five or six, seeing my dad about to go off to work in Limoges hospital. He looked smart and clean-shaven and I asked him, 'Why do you shave before you go to work, Dad?' He told me that he shaved because he wanted to look professional and send the right first impression to his patients when he entered the room. He wanted his patients to look at him and think he looks clean, tidy, professional and as if he's good at his job. He told me that you've got to show that you can look after yourself before you can look after other people.

Limoges is a small city in rural France and it became known for the wrong reasons in the early twentieth century. The story goes that after the defeats by the advancing German army in 1914, a number of senior French military officers deemed incompetent were sent to Limoges so they'd be *out of the way*. And so the word '*Limoger*' was born. It's not dissimilar from being sent to Coventry, only it wasn't a metaphor! Limoges is a unique place – it's rural, working class, left wing and feels a bit detached from the rest of France. When I was growing up, people in their seventies or eighties, who'd been living in the countryside all their life, would come to the hospital, and for some of them, it might have been their first and only time in the hospital or even in the 'city'. They'd often speak patois (more officially called Occitan) rather than French as their first language. There was one guy my dad told me about, who was petrified of being in hospital, and when my dad came into his room, he held the sheet up so it covered him all the way up to his eyes. Dad instantly clocked how he must be feeling and said: '*Covai, grandpa?*' (patois for 'How are you, grandpa?'). As soon as the old man heard that, the sheet came down and he smiled. My dad had connected with him in a way that made him feel welcome and safe. Dad didn't need to think about what he was doing or saying – he'd had so much experience that he knew immediately what was needed in that situation. That is the very spirit of hospitality.

My parents were proud to be nurses. Patient care was everything to them and they wanted to be the best at what they did. They'd tell me that one day we're all going to be like that seventy-something man, and we'd all want to be treated with kindness and respect. We expect the best so we must deliver the best for other people. So, you see, my experience working in hospitality didn't really start at twenty. It was something that I was brought up with, and that my parents taught me. It became part of me subconsciously. My parents planted the seeds and it just grew inside me. Recently my mum said to me: 'We do the same job. We look after people. The only difference is that when I look after them, they're in pain. When you look after them, they're having fun.'

The one thing that unites Brits of all classes is that they're the masters of the understatement. At first, the understatement was synonymous with the upper classes – senior army officers, gentlemen travellers, those kind of folks – but over time it fed down into all of society. And while it became a common language to the Brits, understatement had a habit of causing problems when communicating with someone who wasn't British. One example was during the Korean War in 1951 when a British army officer was on the telephone to his superior officer, an American general. A force of around 600 British soldiers, who were blocking the invasion route to Seoul, was being attacked on all sides by up to 30,000 Chinese troops. Here's what the British brigadier said:

'Things are pretty sticky down there, sir.'

A fellow Brit would have understood this to mean 'Send in your reinforcements'. But an American would be thinking 'That doesn't sound too bad – it seems like they're on top of things!' The 600 Brits held out for four days, before being overrun. Only thirty-nine escaped. I told this story to a British friend recently, only I got the line slightly wrong. Instead of saying 'Things are pretty sticky down there', I said: 'We're in a bit of a pickle.' I wondered which of the two expressions conveyed more urgency, so I asked him. He thought long and hard. '"We're in a bit of a pickle" is worse,' he said, 'because the brigadier is acknowledging more directly that there's a problem.' *Directly? – are you having a laugh, mate?!* I thought. It made me want to compile a sliding scale of British euphemisms for foreigners so they could identify what's a mild inconvenience and what refers to the end of civilisation as we know it.

British understatement is different from the 'stiff upper lip' attitude because it's not just about not wanting to display emotion or spread panic – it's laced with humour in the face of a disastrous situation. There are other examples in British history. Take the Battle of Waterloo in 1815. Lord Uxbridge was in charge of the British heavy cavalry. Towards the end of one of the bloodiest days, Uxbridge was on horseback near the Duke of Wellington, the commander of the Allied forces. Uxbridge was suddenly hit by a cannon ball in his right leg, which was completely blown away. He looked down at where his leg had been and said to Wellington: 'By God, sir, I've lost my leg!' Wellington replied: 'By God, sir, so you have!'

In the 1870s, Dr David Livingstone was trying to find the source of the River Nile. He'd been struck down with both malaria and dysentery, had foot ulcers which meant he couldn't walk and was bleeding heavily internally. He was at death's door, basically. Here's what he wrote in his private diary: 'It is not *all* pleasure, this exploration.'

British understatement was still going strong in the twentieth century when the *Titanic* sank off the coast of Newfoundland in 1912. This is how survivor Cosmo Duff-Gordon (you can't make that name up) summed it up afterwards: 'It was a rather serious evening.' In 1982, a British Airways Boeing 747 unknowingly flew into a volcanic ash cloud over Malaysia. One by one, all four engines failed and the cabin plunged into complete darkness and eerie silence. Captain Eric Moody found the time to make an announcement that went: 'Ladies and gentlemen, this is your captain speaking. We have a small problem. All four engines have stopped. We are doing our damnedest to get them going again. I trust you are not in too much distress.' (Captain Moody did do his damnedest and brought the plane down safely, in case you're wondering.)

The uniquely British dark sense of humour often has me laughing out loud. It's almost like trench humour. You're in the most horrific of situations imaginable and you laugh at it. Part of the reason I find it so funny is because it's so gloriously inconsistent with how Brits usually behave. It also manages to be both inappropriate and completely on point. I remember a guy nearly severing his finger in a kitchen accident and he was laughing while he was telling me how he did it, with his finger almost in two parts. I've never had conversations like this in France. I think Brits reach a tipping point where suddenly everything seems so dire that they abandon their usual reserve and just think *Well – what's the worst that could happen now?* I encountered another example only recently. One car had shunted into another at a set of traffic lights and knocked the car in front past the lights and up a kerb so the left-hand side of the car was on the grass. The guy in the car was fine and got out but a pedestrian walking past said: 'You can't park there, mate!' The guy who said it laughed, but then so did the guy who'd just got out of the car! I couldn't believe it.

What I've come to realise is that there's a whole other language at work within the English language. When you come here, you learn how to speak English. But it takes living here to learn how the Brits actually communicate. Brits downplay all sorts of things in everyday conversations because they don't want to appear rude. For instance, it took me some years to realise that 'It's not quite what I had in mind' doesn't mean that at all. It's more like: 'What the hell is that?!' Likewise, there are some phrases that you need to be on the lookout for because they're secretly telling you that there's an emergency – only you would have no idea from the sound of it. I'm talking about 'It's not ideal', which translates as 'Something terrible has just happened'.

Conversely, while Brits are kings of the understatement, they are also kings of wild exaggeration. It took me a while to realise that 'It's a bloody nightmare' tends to mean 'It's slightly inconvenient'. You miss your Tube in London by a few seconds: 'Bloody nightmare' a Brit might mutter to themselves. I love the fact they say this when there's another Tube in two minutes. The Brits convey their frustration with short phrases, but the French go for noises, typically accompanied by gestures. And we really have mastered noises that convey information, from laissez-faire indifference to pure outrage. '*Bof*', with a shrug of the shoulders, is a great one. It's quite punchy as an expression, and maybe that's one of the reasons why it feels like the French are more in your face compared to the Brits. 'How was the film?' '*Bof*.' It conveys apathy and mild disappointment, or somewhere in the middle – it's average, it's insipid. It's not good, it's not bad, it's ... *Bof*! It's quite a useful expression because if a friend responds with '*Bof*' to a question about how the cinema was, I know what they're saying: wait until the film comes out on Netflix.

'*Aïe aïe aïe*' is another good French expression that you've probably heard, maybe when you see a French sportsperson on television. You also hear it a lot if you work in hospitality, especially if you've got a French chef in the kitchen. *Aïe* actually means 'ouch' and the expression conveys either frustration or mild pain, or both. It's what you'd say if you'd just got a paper cut. '*Pfff*' just sounds like a kind of dramatic exhalation, but it does actually mean something in France. It conveys that you've just heard something that sounds ridiculous or slightly irritating.

Even the way French people say '*Non*' – it's not so much the word, it's the emphasis that matters. '*Non*' is much more punchy, assertive and abrupt than 'No'. President Jacques Chirac said '*Non*' many times in his political career but he most famously used it when asked if France would join the coalition that intended to send troops to Iraq in 2003. The '*Non*' was direct and emphatically clear, and like French noises, it conveyed a lot of information. It became part of how France is perceived around the world.

The British try as hard as possible to avoid saying 'No'. They'd rather form a sentence with a euphemism to spare people’s feelings. Let’s say you’ve just been shown a presentation, and it wasn’t good. ‘Did you like the presentation?’ A Brit isn’t going to say ‘No’ to that even if it was dreadful. Your instinct is to be considerate, so you’ll say something kind like: ‘Er, could we possibly revisit it please?’ or: ‘That was ... interesting.’ The thing is, the person being criticised knows what they’re actually being told and yet the way the news is phrased does provide comfort. This Frenchman doesn’t play by the rules, though. So if a Brit says to me ‘It’s not quite what I had in mind’, I tend to find it funny and might say: ‘I know what you’re saying – you hate it!’ The trouble with that approach is that even then a Brit will want to cushion the blow, opting for something like: ‘No, no, it just needs a little smoothing in places.’ In my experience, Brits are relentlessly sensitive to other people’s feelings, and it’s fascinating compared with the French. The French get what they want and quicker, but there’s a patient compassion about the Brits that I admire. *Vive la différence!*

Despite the decades I’ve lived here, the British behavioural quirks still surprise and delight me, none more so than the British attitude towards the sun. If the temperature rises above about 12°C, which happens around the middle of March, the shorts come on! Brits know that the warmth isn't going to be around for ever, so they make the most of the opportunity they have. And when the sun goes down and they realise that it's actually really cold, they'll stick with the shorts. It's that unique stubborn optimism even in the face of defeat. It reminds me of the Black Knight in *Monty Python and the Holy Grail* who continues to fight a duel with no arms. 'It's just a flesh wound!' It's a similar deal with convertible cars. For years, especially in the late 1990s and 2000s, the Brits bought far more convertible cars than the French, Spanish and Italians. In fact the UK was dubbed 'the convertible capital of Europe' for a time and I love how much this says about the UK. You guys will soak up every single ray of sunshine. And even if the weather's terrible, what do you guys care? You'll still be barbecuing in the rain and driving that convertible.

One thing I had no idea about until late in 2023 was the British attitude towards farting. In many intimate relationships, when someone farts, both people will pretend it never happened. It's just too awkward for the Brits and they can't cope. This was a revelation to me. In France, we fart. It can be loud, it can be smelly, and both partners will typically laugh when it happens. We own our farts. When I was on *I'm a Celebrity*, in the jungle, I farted, quite loudly. I mean, we were basically just eating beans, as we had done for days, and it needed to come out. The former boxer Tony Bellew looked at me and said: 'You're disgusting, mate! I thought you French were all elegant and sophisticated and you're sitting here farting!' I said, in the words of my grandfather: 'It's better to fart in society than to die alone.' Tony wasn't impressed. I should have known. I've spent a lot of time with Gordon and Gino and I realise now our attitude towards farting is very different. I'll fart when I need to. Gino would probably say he farts with style. But Gordon never farts. So maybe I've found one Brit in a million, because Fruitcake and I both fart in each other's company. And we laugh the house down!

4

'They're Too Reserved'

I don't think Brits are as shy and reserved as the French think they are. I think it takes Brits time to acclimatise, and that's no bad thing. In private, after you sit down and have a meaningful conversation, Brits become more and more open. They just need the right environment to feel comfortable. That's what pubs are for!

I know I've written a lot about *Liberté, Égalité, Fraternité* and how huge a part it plays in French history and culture. So, imagine my surprise when these words rang just as true to me in a British pub as they had done in France. A pub is a place where anyone's welcome, social rank doesn't exist and people of all backgrounds come together in harmony. A duke can sit next to a dustman, they can clink their glasses together, smile and say 'Cheers'. It's a place of both celebration and consolation. It's part of the fabric of society and British cultural identity.

The pub is the social hub of a community. People go there for a drink, but really it's more about the socialising than the drinking. There's no equivalent to the pub in France. The closest thing we have in terms of national belonging is the bistro – an intimate, informal type of neighbourhood restaurant – but you're not going to socialise there with people you don't know from the table next door. In the UK, you order your beer and often get chatting to strangers at the bar. You can go there on your own and you feel at home. You feel like you're in familiar surroundings. It's the very spirit of hospitality: warmth and welcome awaits you, and it's built into the foundations.

In Wood Green, north London, I used to go to a pub called the Duke of Edinburgh. I'd head there with friends and we'd have a couple of pints, share some crisps and play some pool. It was an old-school boozer, full of regulars who'd been going there for decades. I'd spend all of Sunday afternoons there with my friends. I loved that place and the conversations you'd have with people that you might never have met if it weren't for the pub. I understood and enjoyed that it was fun to beat the Frenchman at pool. When I first went into the Duke, I was a total stranger and felt like the odd one out. I went in again the next day, and by closing time, I was being treated like a regular.

Everything happens at a slower pace inside a pub. Outside, you have the hustle and bustle of London, but inside, you've found a sanctuary. When my dad comes over to the UK to visit, almost the first thing we do is head to the pub for a pint.

He doesn't speak English, but suddenly he's a pint in and it feels like he can speak all the languages in the world and can converse with anyone. He loves how egalitarian it is and how you feel at home straight away. The French look up to the British pub and admire it. When you're in a pub, you feel like you're right at the heart of British culture, and it's a joyous place to be. You open the door and you can hear everyone talking or laughing. It's such a free, open space that brings people together. For Brits, when they're in France, they want to head to the *boulangerie*. When they're in Britain, the French want to head to the pub.

After a while, you appreciate that pubs come in lots of different forms and attract different crowds. There are the country pubs, and they can be intimate, unassuming spaces just by the roadside or vast places hidden away in former grand houses with gardens, rivers, bridges and streams. In cities, there are the old-school traditional pubs that attract an older crowd, and the cool places under railway arches and in converted industrial estates that tend to appeal to a younger crowd. There are the pubs that have been gentrified and those that absolutely resist that. Not long after I'd arrived in the UK in the 1990s, the gastropub came along.

It was a total game-changer because the one thing you wouldn't get in an old-school pub was a quality meal. You'd get stodgy staples that just about did the job or no food at all. But the gastropub managed to combine the hospitality and heritage of the pub with the kind of quality home-cooked cuisine you'd find in a French bistro. It was a gamble at the time but it was a match made in heaven. Fast-forward to now and it's exciting to see pubs doing things differently, like the Prince of Peckham, set up by local resident Clement Ogbonnaya just off Peckham High Street. He wanted to create a community venue that reflects and attracts the diverse community it serves, and Peckham is as diverse as they come. Clement's mastered it. Gastropub quality with Jamaican flavours. So you'll get fried chicken supreme and jerk pork belly as his interpretation of a Sunday roast. And the place is packed.

The pubs in Mayfair, near Le Gavroche, used to fascinate me, because the Monopoly board isn't lying – Mayfair is one the poshest and most expensive areas in the country. The assumption is that you're not going to find a place to drink or eat that's affordable. But it's not true – there are inexpensive restaurants like the fantastic Madrid-inspired tapas place El Pirata, which has been there for twenty-five years and serves delicious food at incredible value for money. There are still neighbourhood boozers; the only giveaway that you're in a fancy locale is that the bathrooms and furnishings are a little swankier. In these pubs you find a surprisingly diverse crowd including super-rich residents, people who work in the local offices, and in December tourists who might have stumbled across the pub after checking out Winter Wonderland in Hyde Park.

The British pub is a place for all seasons. In winter, it's a refuge from the cold. There's a roaring fire going and the whole place feels warm, not just from the fire but from the mirth around you. The wood smoke makes you feel like you've gone back in time. Everyone's drinking stout and dark beers. Then, when it gets lighter and warmer again, everyone's on the tables outside drinking pale ales and sipping G&Ts. Wearing those shorts.

One of my favourite pub experiences has been, of course, in the New Forest. One winter a few years ago, I ate an amazing ploughman's lunch in the Royal Oak pub in Fritham. Like a lot of good British country pubs, it's got charm and character. It's a very old and wonderfully crooked place. Higgledy-piggledy is what the Brits would say. The kind of place where you walk along such an uneven floor that it makes you feel like you've had several more pints than you've actually had. Another great pub is the Green Man in the Essex countryside. In summer, in the beer garden, you can end up spending the entire day there. It's an incredible pub, owned by the Galvin brothers (who I used to work with) and they do 200–300 covers on a Sunday. The quality is sensational. People travel some distances to visit but it's full of locals as well. Parts of the building date back to 1341 and it manages to combine the rustic and the modern. It's surrounded by beautiful countryside and even has a river running through the bottom of the garden. It's a vision of Old England and you can't help but feel like you've stepped into paradise. Paradise with a pint.

Britain is where I properly discovered beer. It's no overstatement to say that Britain is producing some of the best beers in the world. Being here in the 2000s for the craft beer revolution was incredible. I became a beer geek and now I'm forever looking for delicious new nectar. I love a pale ale and I'm always on the lookout if I stumble across a beer shop or a farmers' market. Back when I was living in Peckham, I'd go to the Beer Shop in Nunhead (now sadly closed, but they do have one in Folkestone) and invariably come home carrying a few cans and bottles, which I couldn't wait to try. I discovered Cloudwater Brew there, which started in Manchester in 2014, a light and vibrant session ale, full of flavour and very refreshing – and aptly named 'How Wonderful'. It has tropical fruit notes that lead on to a lovely bitterness and a hoppy finish. Who'd have thought twenty years ago that I'd be describing beer like a tasting note for a fine wine?

In my first year here, the stereotype about Brits being too reserved felt like a myth. I found the UK to be really open and warm. People made me feel like I belonged and that's one of the reasons I stayed. In my first couple of years here, my group of friends would often end up at a house party. The best type of house party I went to was a blues party. Blues parties started in the Caribbean in the 1950s but they took off in the 1960s in the UK because black people were being refused entry into clubs and bars. They were basically parties in someone's house where black people could dance and have a good time. Everyone paid an entrance fee to get in and then we danced to roots, reggae and bashment all night. I loved blues parties before we'd even walked through the door. That was partly because I've been a big Bob Marley fan since I discovered his music, aged sixteen. Something about the beat of reggae music is so appealing – I think maybe it's the antidote to the fast-paced way I live the rest of my life. It also taps into my rebellious, anti-establishment spirit.

At house parties, I spent most of the time chatting in the kitchen, because everybody seemed so curious about me. They wanted to hear my story, about how I had ended up here. When people found out I was the maître d' at a restaurant where a lot of celebrities went, they wanted to know who I'd met and what they were like in real life. It was just so different from most people's experience of working in an office with a similar routine each day. It's true that you never know what's going to happen in a restaurant. That's one of the reasons it's such an exciting place to be. Yes, you start early, finish late and only have a short break in the afternoon, but it's a dynamic and diverse way to earn a living because of the sheer number of people you get to meet.

I noticed that Brits weren't reserved when it came to wanting to learn about me or other people. What they did seem reserved about was opening up about themselves, and I could see after a while that it wasn't because they were stand-offish. It came from a place of shyness, born out of self-deprecation and humility. Brits don't want to come across like they're bragging or making too much noise about themselves. They get self-conscious. The same thing happens when you try and pay a Brit a compliment. I can't tell you the number of times on *First Dates* that a Brit has gone red, looked away, or smiled very shyly when I've paid them a compliment. Or the number of times when I say something along the lines of 'I like your dress' and the person responds: 'Oh, this old thing?!' to deflect the attention away. It's almost like there are unwritten rules that you're not allowed to break. It's so liberating not having to follow the rules, and that's one of my privileges as a Frenchman with a rebellious streak.

I was on a podcast with Tom Kerridge recently and he asked me what the food that I'd cooked in the jungle on *I'm a Celebrity* was like. I said: 'It was unbelievable, if I may say so myself.' And he looked at me, laughed, and said: 'Well, that's modest, Fred!' But I stand by it – it *was* unbelievable! I know it's a big faux pas in the UK to praise something you've made or done. Brits can't be seen to celebrate themselves, especially in a way that's perceived to be really emphatic. I wonder what it would be like if Brits did have that freedom. Imagine a situation where a rugby player (from any of the nations in the UK) has just delivered the best performance of their career and the post-match interviewer asks: 'How do you think you played today?' Instead of saying 'Yeah, it was a decent performance, I'm just pleased that we got the win today', which is what a Brit would typically say, deflecting the attention away from themselves, they answer: 'I was fantastic today. Absolutely on fire.'

It's never happened, and it never will!

As a foreigner, I get to play by different rules. I don't have to worry about sounding pretentious. If I think what I've done or made is utter crap, I'll have no mercy with myself and no problem telling everyone. Equally, if I think it's unbelievable, I'm going to say it! My dad's the same. I remember seeing him putting on a new suit one Sunday many years ago. We went to a restaurant for lunch and the waiter said: 'You're looking very dapper today.' My dad responded by opening the jacket so the waiter could see the jazzy lining, turned slightly so that he was facing him at a 45° angle, and said: '*Un rien m'habille*' ('I look good in anything'), and smiled. My dad was both having a laugh and being deadly serious. He knows he looks good in the suit and he's telling the waiter *thanks for noticing*!

Brits are worried about how they come across, how people are going to perceive them and what people are going to think. They're very polite and very respectful and don't want to offend anybody. Put all of this together and you can see why Brits are often labelled with adjectives like 'shy' and 'reserved' by people from other countries. When you compare them to the publicly and obviously extroverted French or Italians, for example, there is some truth in these labels. But being a bit reserved does give the Brits an advantage in some ways. While the French tend to make it clear how they're feeling, the Brits tend to hold back. And that gives them an air of mystery, or intrigue, which can be very attractive.

But some Brits are as far away from 'reserved' as it's possible to be – I'm talking about the legendary British eccentrics. Every country has their eccentrics, but Brits do eccentricity better than anyone else. Maybe it's because it's a trait that is typically celebrated here. Why shouldn't it be? Eccentricity is associated with creativity, originality, humour, intelligence, quirkiness and not wanting to be told what to do, and I'm on board with all of these things. Genius inventor Alan Turing was known to be witty and charming but he was impatient and liked things a particular way. During World War II, when he was working at Bletchley Park trying to crack the German Enigma code, he would sometimes be summoned to meetings at the Foreign Office in central London. He was a keen long-distance runner and didn't like public transport, so sometimes he'd run the forty miles to get there. He loved running and could easily run that far, so why not? Eccentrics dare to do things differently and don't fit into a traditional mould. Many of them are icons in Britain, like Stephen Fry, Grayson Perry, Helena Bonham Carter and Vivienne Westwood.

Even the place names are eccentric in Britain. You just have to drive through the Cotswolds, the High Weald of Kent, Norfolk or Devon and you'll come across villages with the most extraordinary names. Places like Giggleswick, Great Snoring, Nether Wallop, Barton in the Beans, West Wittering and Lower Dicker. They're quirky, unique and you can't pass through them without laughing. Maybe that was the effect they were after – to put people in a good mood when they see the sign on the road. And to make matters more eccentric, some of these places aren't pronounced remotely like they're spelled. That took some getting used to for me as a Frenchman, and I'm still cracking the code thirty-two years later. Some of them, like Marylebone and Holborn, you learn quickly if you're living in London. But these are entry level compared to places like Trottiscliffe (pronounced 'Troz-lee') in Kent and Cholmondeley (pronounced 'Chum-lee') in Cheshire. And then there are the place names that are fool's gold to a Frenchman, because they're formed from French words. So, of course, I felt confident that 'Belvoir' would be pronounced Bel-voir. Nope. It's 'Beaver'. Are you having a laugh?! Then you've got some of that gloriously British inconsistency, because Beaulieu in the New Forest is pronounced 'Bew-ley' but Beauchief, in South Yorkshire, is pronounced 'Bee-chiff'. Family names follow a similarly ridiculous pattern. 'Featherstonehaugh' would be hard enough to pronounce even if it obeyed the rules, but when someone tells you it's pronounced 'Fanshaw', you wonder if you're being wound up. You can't make this stuff up and I adore it.

Brits enjoy pastimes and festivals that they don't realise are as unusual and unique as they are. Birdwatching is a good example. Britain is a nation of birdwatchers. The Royal Society for the Protection of Birds is the largest bird organisation in Europe and has over a million members. As soon as some rare species of bird is spotted in the Outer Hebrides or on the coast of Northumberland, twitchers load all sorts of expensive equipment into the back of the car and they leave within the hour, like they're on some kind of James Bond spy mission. A good friend of mine, Erik, fits into this category. We go walking together in the Kent Downs and we met up recently at Chartwell, the beautiful former home of Winston Churchill, now looked after by the National Trust. We met in the car park and Erik was kitted out like a nineteenth-century gentleman explorer. He had his walking boots on, a green wax jacket, green corduroy trousers, a stick, a compass, a pair of binoculars, even an old-school printed map. Of course, after about an hour, despite his supreme confidence, we got lost. 'You should have packed your flare gun, Erik!' I thought. It took us ten minutes to realise where we were – we'd managed to get lost in a park. I ribbed him mercilessly and we laughed and laughed. As much as I tease Erik about twitching and as much as he teases me about how Frenchmen seem to be obsessed with a different type of bird, I have become more and more British over the years. And one of the things I love now is listening to the dawn chorus of songbirds.

To be fair, birdwatching is mainstream compared to some of the wackier British hobbies. The Cooper's Hill Cheese-Rolling contest involves chasing a four-kilogram round of Double Gloucester cheese down a ridiculously steep hill in Gloucestershire. No one cares that people have broken their legs and arms trying to win. In 2023, the winner of the ladies' race, Delaney Irving, managed to win the race despite falling on her head and being knocked out. She actually only discovered she'd won when she woke up in the medical tent.

Then there's the Wife-Carrying Race in Dorking, Surrey. The competitors can be male or female and they carry a 'wife' (who can be male or female, and doesn't actually need to be married to the person carrying them) over a distance of just under 400 metres. Apparently, there are only six permitted 'wife-carrying positions' and if the 'wife' weighs under fifty kilos, the competitor has to wear a rucksack filled with flour to make up the required weight. I love how an event that sounds like something out of a Monty Python sketch is taken so seriously. I've mentioned the idea to Fruitcake a few times but she's not biting. I'm working on it.

Let's not forget Wales and the World Bog Snorkelling Championship, held annually since

1976 in Llanwrtyd Wells. Competitors have to wear snorkels, masks and flippers, and complete two consecutive lengths of a 55-metre-long water-filled trench cut through a peat bog. They're not allowed to use swimming strokes – they can only use 'flipper power'. Scotland has the World Stone-Skimming Championship, held on the little Hebridean island of Easdale, seventeen miles from Oban. It takes place in a flooded quarry and the slate found naturally on the island is perfect skimming material. Each competitor is allowed three skims and many entrants choose a pun-based alias, like 'Skimminy Cricket' and the 'Real Skim Shady'.

Eccentricity is even built into the official traditions of the UK. Each year, the official State Opening of Parliament takes place. Before this can happen, the Yeomen of the Guard – a bodyguard of the monarch originally created in 1485 – search the cellars at the Palace of Westminster in case they find anyone trying to blow up the place, like Guy Fawkes back in 1605. As a legacy of the English Civil War and the execution of King Charles I in 1649, the monarch also 'kidnaps' an MP and holds them hostage at Buckingham Palace while he or she is delivering the King's/Queen's Speech. Before the speech can take place, 'Black Rod' (the monarch's representative in the House of Lords, whose name derives from the ebony staff they carry) has to knock on the door to the Chamber of the House of Commons. Then they have the door shut in their face three times to symbolise the independence of the House of Commons.

Then there's the ritual when a new Speaker of the House of Commons is elected. Historically, no one wanted the job because Speakers tended to lose their heads if they offended the monarch, so they needed more than a little persuasion to take up the position. As a ceremonial nod to that, the successful candidate these days is still physically dragged to the chair by two MPs. You can't make all this stuff up!

And it doesn't stop here. The day-to-day activities of Parliament are equally eccentric. When a bill (a proposed law) is sent from the House of Commons for the House of Lords to debate, the clerk writes 'Soit bail as Seigneurs' (Let it be sent to the Lords) in Norman French and ties it up elaborately with green ribbon. It's funny to see the French represented at the heart of the British establishment! And until 2017, when a proposed law became a law, it wasn't written on paper but on vellum (calfskin), which costs an arm and a leg.

MPs don't vote on bills by pushing an electronic button or signing a piece of paper – they have to walk through two narrow corridors. It doesn't get any easier when they come back to their seats in the House of Commons, because while there are 650 MPs, there are actually only seats for 427 people.

That's why you see so many people standing up near the entrance to the Chamber, especially at Prime Minister's Questions, which is something I really enjoy. It feels like an intellectual boxing bout, where an unexpected punch can completely flatten an opponent and change the mood of the entire Chamber. MPs have to creatively argue without resorting to explicitly insulting language or coming across as 'unparliamentary'. Fellow MPs have to be referred to as 'honourable friends' or 'right honourable friends' and that means allegations, put-downs, jibes and turns of phrase are so politely and elegantly framed, they're almost works of art. But to be fair, that is almost exactly what regular Brits do every day with their euphemisms and wordplay to avoid directly offending people. It's so wonderfully and uniquely British.

The French are supposed to be the ones known for showing how they feel, but Brits feel just as much!

If you don't know all the things that are going on inside the head of Brits, yes, they might come across as reserved. But once you get to know them, you realise that what you're seeing might be the tip of an iceberg that's miles deep.

Let's get back to complaining, for example. Fruitcake and I are like chalk and cheese over some things, and it makes us laugh. Like most Brits, she can be quite reserved and it takes a lot for her to make a complaint. She'd need to be really unhappy about something. I've talked to British friends about this and it seems Brits need to get more annoyed than they actually are to give them the confidence to complain, so they work themselves up. It starts with the thought: 'Should I say something?' and if they can answer yes in their heads, it becomes the more confident thought: 'I should say something.' But that's still not quite enough to convince them to complain yet. They need to think it over a little more before the confidence swells and they can finally announce: 'I'm going to say something!' It's almost like Brits have to fill an imaginary vase until it's overflowing. When it does, that's when the complaint happens. And then the relief felt is huge. The whole process from initial disappointment to resolution is an emotional roller coaster over the course of anything up to half an hour that covers self-doubt, apprehension, courage, relief and joy. It's as if Brits experience an entire play inside their heads.

My practice when it comes to complaining is more like this: experience disappointment, voice disappointment, reach contentment. There's a problem and a solution. It's fast, simple and logical. Even so, Fruitcake's natural instinct when I'm about to say something is to get embarrassed because I've gone and done it again – Fred's said what he felt! It's like the French approach is jumping in at the deep end rather than the British approach of inching in from the shallow end. Both approaches reach the same outcome – you end up in the pool! But while jumping in at the deep end does make you more comfortable more quickly, I can see the appeal of the shallow end. It's a slow, patient and painstaking (verging on slightly masochistic) process and I understand now that this is what the Brits are all about. Queuing, cricket, gardening and waiting for that cup of tea to brew are all exercises in patience. But when something finally happens – whether it's reaching the front gates of Wimbledon after queuing all night, finally taking that wicket after spending three hours fielding, that moment when the roses bloom in June, or sitting down for a cup of tea of just the right colour and temperature, the pay-off is magnificent. When that happens, the Brits aren't just excited – they're completely euphoric!

5

'They've Got No Style'

The French think they are way more stylish than the British. We all have that image in our minds of a Frenchwoman looking effortlessly elegant and fashionable, maybe in a black-and-white A-line dress on the banks of the River Seine. The trouble is, as hard as I've looked, I've never actually found this woman! That's because both the French and the Brits (and the rest of the world) are in love with an image from a bygone era – an iconic image that passed from memory into myth. A stereotype now detached from its source. But it's in France's interests to keep selling the myth and, as luck would have it, everyone still wants to buy it. France is the mannequin that everyone looks up to. As self-deprecating Brits, you think you're in her shadow. But you're not. Brits sell themselves seriously short on style. Britain might well be the birthplace of menswear and still has the finest tailors in the world. Brits have introduced the dinner jacket, the three-piece suit, the trench coat, the riding coat, brogues and the bowler hat. In the twentieth century, Brits brought the world the miniskirt, mod style and punk fashion. We're still wearing these things. I've been to both the Paris and London Fashion Weeks and the energy, variety and innovation of the London one is on another level. And it's the same when you're walking down Oxford Street or the King's Road – you notice how many different styles people are wearing. Brits have been fashion pioneers for generations. You just don't give yourselves the credit for it.

When I was working at Le Gavroche, sometimes in the break we'd get between lunch and dinner, I'd walk around Mayfair. One day, I wandered down Chesterfield Street, which looks like something out of a Jane Austen novel, and I noticed that one of the houses had two blue plaques on it. The first of them was for Anthony Eden, the prime minister in the mid-1950s, which sounded like the right calibre of resident in this posh part of town. The second plaque was for a person by the name of Beau Brummell. As a Frenchman, someone with the name 'Beau' ('Beautiful') is going to catch your eye. Then I looked under his name on the plaque, where it tells you what the commemorated person did for a living. It just said 'Leader of Fashion'. I thought *Wow – this guy must have been something!*

It transpires that at the start of the nineteenth century this address was the most fashionable place in Britain. George (nicknamed 'Beau') Brummell had been an officer in the personal regiment of the Prince of Wales. Brummell's charm and grace stood out, as did his habit of accessorising any item of clothing, so the two struck up an unlikely friendship. In 1799, Brummell turned twenty-one and bought a house with his inheritance on Chesterfield Street. On most mornings, the Prince of Wales turned up to discuss fashion. Brummell was the talk of the town. He loathed the fashion of the day, which was the 'if you've got it, flaunt it' kind of thing. We're talking powdered wigs, lace cravats, loud colours and expensive sparkling trinkets. Beau favoured perfectly tailored clothing and muted colours. He wore dark coats and trousers rather than breeches. And the *pièce de résistance* was his perfectly knotted cravat. He even sent them to be laundered and starched in the countryside, where the air smelled more fragrant. He washed every day (unheard of in those days) so, unlike every other gentleman, he didn't have to apply litres of perfume to cover his odour, because he was clean!

Beau was the original 'dandy' and might have been the first fashion influencer. His own style was inspired by two fashionable aristocratic groups in Paris that had survived the French Revolution: the Muscadins and the Incroyables. But Beau combined his favourite elements and incorporated them into his own unique look, which was so popular that the French imported it back. It's all part of the great unspoken cultural exchange that has peppered the relationship between our two nations over the last few centuries. We've just been so busy fighting, antagonising or getting one up on each other that we weren't able to acknowledge it at the time. Now we can. And we can also see that the periods of conflict actually helped define some of the qualities and skills that we most admire in each other.

Savile Row became famous around the world for its bespoke tailoring, but it never would have happened without the French. Let me rephrase that – it never would have happened if it hadn't been for *fighting the French*. If Napoleon Bonaparte hadn't been hell-bent on conquering Europe, the British wouldn't have been at war with France. War with France meant that hundreds of young aristocratic military officers needed their uniforms made. But being an army officer meant you didn't just need a uniform – you needed an entire bespoke wardrobe of dress suits and lounge wear. Savile Row just happened to be the address of many of the senior officers in the British army. At that point in time, tailors would travel to the customer, so dozens of them were going in and out of the prestigious addresses on Savile Row. Eventually it made sense for the tailors to set up shops nearby. In 1803, Savile Row had its first tailor's shop. In 1846, the tailor Henry Poole moved in. And he's still there. Well, his shop is, at number 15. Henry Poole's a big deal because he's the guy who came up with the dinner jacket.

After a period of decline, Savile Row regained its prestige again in the 1960s through designer Tommy Nutter, known as 'the rebel on the row'. He was the guy who gave John, Paul and Ringo their famous look that features on the cover of *Abbey Road*. Britain successfully reinvented itself during the Swinging Sixties. It was suddenly the place to be – the coolest, most stylish place on the planet. The list of bands that burst onto the scene between 1960 and 1965 is like a *Who's Who* of music: the Beatles, the Who, the Kinks, Pink Floyd and the Rolling Stones. It was the sound of a new generation. Britain was ruling the waves on every front. England even won the World Cup! Everyone was talking about London's Carnaby Street and King's Road as the fashion hot spots of the world. Before I came to Britain, I was desperate to see the King's Road. My friend who got me the job at La Tante Claire had told me all about it. It was the ultimate place to watch the world go by, with its beautiful, fashionable people, fancy cars, boutiques and restaurants. It was where the cool kids were at. In the cinema, Britain was producing the films everyone wanted to see. James Bond was three films in by 1964 and *Goldfinger* was a worldwide phenomenon.

In 2012, when I was the maître d' at Galvin at Windows on Park Lane, Daniel Craig came in with his wife Rachel Weisz. It was only a few weeks after he'd appeared as James Bond with the Queen in that incredible scene in the London 2012 Olympics opening ceremony, so that memory was still very fresh in my mind. I greeted and welcomed them as soon as they arrived in the restaurant, and gave them the best table in the house, overlooking Hyde Park. Inside I was all of a flutter, squealing: 'Oh my God – James Bond is here!' After that iconic moment in the opening ceremony, it was like we had royalty in the restaurant. I was looking after the absolute *crème de la crème* – what an honour. I set up their seats facing the windows so no one could see who they were from behind and bother them. They'd arrived really early and there were no other guests around so I asked them if they'd like to have a look at the view from the balcony, which is pretty spectacular.

You can only access the balcony through the kitchen so I led the way. The kitchen staff could not believe their eyes when Daniel Craig entered, dressed immaculately, oozing charm and confidence. Seeing as a restaurant kitchen is a classic location for so many movie shootouts and chases, it basically felt like we'd all been transported to a film set. Everyone was completely mesmerised. Suddenly Daniel reached inside his suit jacket, and something metallic dropped to the floor. Everyone in the kitchen was thinking the same thing: has he dropped his gun?! It was his mobile phone. But even then, we were thinking *Is that just a mobile phone – or is it really a mini rocket launcher?!*

The French adore James Bond. We don't have an equivalent fictional secret agent in France, and we don't need one, because James Bond is perfect as he is. We love how British he is, with his politeness, discretion, charm, humour, unflappability and his beautiful British cars, but we're also secretly quite proud of how much he likes the French way of life. His favourite drink is champagne, he speaks French fluently, he much prefers coffee to tea, his favourite card game is baccarat, and if you think about the classic Bond film location, it tends to be a casino on the French Riviera.

The 1960s was a time for the French to leave behind the years of post-war hardship. My parents were both born just after World War II, and while they didn't experience the harsh realities of wartime France, life in the late 1940s didn't just go back to how it used to be. Over a million buildings had been destroyed or badly damaged and there was still a thriving black market. Rationing was still in place and violent protests broke out in 1947 because of the lack of food. Things only started to get better after the American Marshall Plan began to provide aid to France, in 1948. The 1950s was a time of gradual rebuilding, paving the way for a time of plenty and prosperity in the 1960s. My dad told me many times that during the sixties, you could quit one job at midday and find another job by 2 p.m. There was so much work going on.

My mum and dad met when they were both sixteen, in 1963. Rock 'n' roll had reached France some years before that, but not without reservation. And that's because France wanted to do what it usually does – dance to its own beat. So the French created their own unique style of pop music, which became known as '*yé-yé*' (named after all the 'yeah yeah' choruses in American and British rock 'n' roll songs). The French wanted to ensure that French music didn't get completely swept away by what was happening elsewhere so everything was sung in French, almost entirely by French musicians. Artists like Françoise Hardy and Sylvie Vartan became household names, and the songwriter behind many of the biggest hits was Serge Gainsbourg. But some British actresses and singers became big parts of the *yé-yé* scene, like Gillian Hills and Jane Birkin, both of whom appeared in the massively influential film *Blow-Up* in 1966. Birkin and Gainsbourg met in 1969 and, soon after, they'd recorded that legendary song '*Je t'aime ... moi non plus*'.

Yé-yé was born from the desire to conserve and protect French heritage and language. The Brits proudly call English 'the language of Shakespeare', but the French are just as proud of their own language, which we call '*la langue de Molière*'. And when the French language takes the world stage, like it does during the Olympics, the French beam with pride. They'll stop at nothing to protect their language. In 1994, the French government introduced a law that stipulates at least 40 per cent of the music played on French radio stations must be in French. For many young people, like me, it felt inward-looking and conservative at a time in our lives where we wanted to see what the world had to offer.

What's all this got to do with the British sense of style? you might be wondering. The point is, the Brits seemed much more open-minded about seeking inspiration from abroad. Take the mods, for example. They were obsessed with French and Italian suits, but they added their unique British twists, like the Royal Air Force roundel symbol, which famously became the logo of the Who, the band that moulded the mods. The RAF actually borrowed the symbol from the French Air Force – it had been introduced during World War I so that troops on the ground could recognise their own planes. The RAF just swapped the colours around, so the blue was on the outside rather than in the centre. In similar fashion, the mods fell in love with Italian Vespas and Lambrettas, but they painted them red, white and blue, and embellished them with mirrors, lights, racks and Union Jacks. While they might have embraced influences from elsewhere, the Brits had a magic touch when it came to curating an ensemble, taking it in exciting new directions and adopting it as part of their culture. The mods became mainstream and their style became an enduring, iconic aesthetic. I've seen the number of scooters heading out of south London to Brighton for the Mod Weekender event in August. It's like you're back in the Swinging Sixties. We're all mods, when you think about it, with our skinny suits, slim ties and parkas.

In November 1962, France and the UK signed a unique treaty that created one of the most incredible and iconic machines of the twentieth century – Concorde, a fashion icon in itself. It was the first time that any two countries had joined forces to construct an aircraft. The Entente Cordiale was back in business! Concorde was the first supersonic passenger-carrying aircraft and it represented the height of style and sophistication. I went inside a Concorde when we were filming the first episode of *The Ultimate Wedding Planner*. The couple wanted to hold the reception under the plane, which was in its own hangar in Manchester Airport. We were all given a tour inside and it's an unbelievable machine – so sleek and so beautiful, if a little short on legroom. The fact that it could travel at 1,320 mph and go from Paris or London to New York in under three hours was incredible. But the project wasn't without its friction between our two nations, which is funny, given that the name of the plane – Concorde – means harmony!

And why did they end up spelling it the French way? The myth is that the French always get their way, but the name was actually suggested by a Brit – the eighteen-year-old son of the publicity manager at British Aircraft Corporation's base near Bristol. Part of the reason he chose it was because 'concord/*concorde*' meant the same in French as it did in English. The plan was for both countries to use the spelling with the 'e', until President de Gaulle insulted Prime Minister Macmillan during a meeting in 1963. Macmillan responded by declaring that he would remove the 'e' from the British spelling of Concorde. It was only put back by Tony Benn, the Minister of Technology, in December 1967, when he travelled to Toulouse to watch the aircraft's first flight. As recorded in the National Archives, he announced: 'From now on the British Concorde will also be spelt with an "e". The letter "E" symbolises many things. "E" stands for excellence, for England, for Europe and for Entente – that alliance of sympathy and affection which binds our two countries together.'

At that time, our two countries were in very different places politically. In the UK, the Labour Party's

Harold Wilson had become the youngest prime minister since the nineteenth century. All sorts of social changes were taking place: capital punishment was abolished, homosexuality was decriminalised and abortion was legalised. Meanwhile, France had a very conservative president in charge and he'd been in power for ten years. Although, for the record, France had decriminalised homosexuality during the French Revolution in 1791! Under de Gaulle, young people felt like they were suffocating in a country completely out of step with the changes happening across the West. Something had to give, and in May 1968, it did.

It all began when restrictions were placed on dormitory visits at the University of Paris that basically prevented male and female students from sleeping together. If you want to start a revolution in France, stopping couples from having sex is a great way to go about it. There was a big protest, students were arrested and part of the university was closed. In a show of solidarity, students at Sorbonne University responded by occupying an amphitheatre, but they were violently dispersed by the Paris police. Huge numbers of students took to the streets. Demonstrations spread to the factories of France and soon to every sector of the French workforce. The country completely ground to a halt. The slogans of May 1968 became part of French national consciousness. *Sous les pavés, la plage!* (Under the pavement, the beach!) was one of the most famous and I love it because you have to take a moment to think about it before realising how beautiful it is. Students and artists had dug up Paris's cobblestones, discovering that sand lay underneath – it was a very powerful metaphor for freedom and rebuilding society from the city's foundations.

The protesters made barricades out of the paving stones and scrawled: '*La barricade ferme la rue mais ouvre la voie*' ('The barricade blocks the street but opens the way'). They wanted a better life and felt that they deserved it. They dreamt they could build a different world with different rules. President de Gaulle was so alarmed that he fled to Germany, which many perceived as cowardice at the time. What he was actually doing was meeting one of his army generals at a military base to talk about the possible intervention of the army. The following day, de Gaulle returned and addressed the nation, calling for citizens to rise up against what he basically termed a Communist insurrection. He also said he'd dissolve parliament and call an election. The following day, nearly a million pro de Gaulle supporters marched through central Paris and the threat of revolution ended. His party won the election convincingly but de Gaulle had been hugely weakened. The appetite for social change couldn't be ignored.

Naturally, my parents were among the student protesters, known proudly as the *soixante-huitards* (the sixty-eights), and in many ways, it's defined their entire lives. They felt that they were realising the unfulfilled dreams of the French Revolution, 180 years later. The slogans from 1968 are still known across France because the plight of the protesters still resonates to this day. People have the posters up in their houses. My mum still says: 'If it wasn't for '68, and what we fought to achieve, we wouldn't be here and you wouldn't be living this life, Fred.' And they're right. They proved that they could change things. The rights of workers changed – wages rose by 10 per cent, the minimum wage increased by 35 per cent, the working week was shortened and employers had to hold consultations before firing employees. The events of 1968 led to the creation of the Women's Liberation Movement, which paved the way for sweeping changes. Philosophy had become a weapon for the working class. They weren't just worthless workers in the factories any more. They were people who thought and aspired to better things. A wind of hedonism was blowing across France. By day, my parents were chanting about workers' rights, and they'd be out dancing all night.

In the UK, the big dreams of the 1960s came crashing down, and out of the ashes, punk was born. Punk might have started in the USA in New York, but it's for ever associated with Britain, partly because it had such a social impact here. Punk is like Britain itself – a melting pot of cultures. Musically it had its roots in ska, which started in Jamaica in the 1950s. And the Windrush generation of Jamaicans brought their music with them when they emigrated to the UK in the 1950s and 60s. The French also had a big impact on British punk. Some of the most significant players, like Malcolm McLaren, were hugely inspired by the situationist movement in France. Some of his and Vivienne Westwood's iconic punk fashion of the 1970s featured slogans from the riots of 1968. Academics have argued that the French put the politics into punk.

I discovered punk when I was twelve years old, when a friend introduced me to the music of the Clash and the Sex Pistols in the mid-1980s. At the time, I was finding French music really dull and frustrating. It wasn't doing anything new; I'd put the radio on and it was French people playing old French music. At home, my dad had a big record collection and the LP player was his pride and joy. But except for a bit of Elvis Presley and a touch of the Beatles, he played almost entirely French music. He loved the French stars of the 1960s and 70s like Françoise Hardy and Johnny Hallyday, who's often referred to as the French Elvis. Johnny played to huge stadiums across Europe and was still topping the charts in his mid-sixties. He rewrote a lot of big English-language hits in French, like 'Hey Joe' and 'House of the Rising Sun', and much of the French public weren't aware that some of his hits were based on English originals. My dad's favourite song is still Hallyday's 'Gabrielle', which was adapted from little-known Australian singer-songwriter Tony Cole's song 'The King is Dead'. The original didn't chart in the UK or US, but Johnny's version in 1976 went to number one in France.

I wanted to hear music with energy and passion – something I felt represented my experience, and not that of my parents. Then I heard the Clash for the first time, and it was a breath of fresh air. Well, more like a blast of fresh air. The Sex Pistols were something else, though. No one had ever heard anything like it. It was completely compelling chaos. Sid Vicious was incredible. Everything about them and their story was just pure anarchy. Sid Vicious wasn't even in the original Sex Pistols line-up but was hired after manager Malcolm McLaren fired bassist Glen Matlock because 'he liked the Beatles'. When the band signed to A&M records, they celebrated by destroying the company's offices. These guys weren't just talking the talk. They were hellraisers.

I branched into heavy metal after that, starting with AC/DC and Led Zeppelin, then moving on to Black Sabbath, Iron Maiden, Motörhead and Mötley Crüe. It felt like I was discovering a totally new genre of music every year. Reggae followed, when I was sixteen.

This period made me realise that there are a lot of different things in the world, and to just focus my energy and enthusiasm on one thing felt like I was short-changing the amazing variety on offer. I don't label myself 'eclectic' because that suggests a kind of intentional order to it. I just like what I like and it just so happens that I like a lot of different things. That was a bit unusual at school, though, where kids were quite tribal about what they liked. I remember a conversation with a guy at my secondary school when I was fifteen and he was super into heavy metal. He had the leather jacket, pins and badges everywhere, skinny jeans, Doc Martens and wild hair, and we started talking about heavy metal. I couldn't afford a leather jacket so I'd bought a denim one with badges and logos on it. But there weren't anywhere near as many badges as there were on his jacket. And I had short hair. He looked at me and said: 'You're not a real hard rocker.' (In French, heavy metal is confusingly called 'hard rock'.) 'You can't be a real hard rocker because you like other music too, so you're not like me.' I thought – it's great that he's so passionate about what he's into, but he's kind of shooting himself in the foot by not even listening to anything else. But he couldn't accept my point of view. To him, it was almost a betrayal. I could never understand that mentality. I would dance to any type of music I liked. It just so happened that everything I thought was good was in English, and that extended to film and TV too. That was what started my fascination with the UK. I wanted to speak English all the time because it was like being in a movie – the movie of my life.

When I was growing up in the 1980s, I felt like all the good edgy fashion and music came from Britain. There was a young generation of Brits who just wanted to burn the rule book, and that struck a chord with me.

The only exception was the aforementioned Serge Gainsbourg. My dad liked the music Gainsbourg wrote earlier in his career – the catchy, middle-of-the-road stuff for the *yé-yé* singers. Serge was a clever composer who understood what it took to create hits and waited until he'd built a successful platform before writing and performing what he really wanted to sing. Then he started to become more experimental and provocative. That's when he lost the interest of people like my dad, but he ignited something in people like me who wanted to hear music that challenged the status quo. My mum was somewhere in the middle. She liked Serge's music but wasn't impressed with him as a person. We'd be watching TV and she'd say '*Dégueulasse!*' (Disgusting!) because Serge was unshaven, his hair was always a mess, he'd usually have a cigarette in his mouth and he'd come out and say something outrageous. He was and is a divisive figure but more people liked him than didn't, and the ones who didn't like him fuelled his notoriety. Either way, you couldn't help but take notice.

Serge made me question why we do what we do and opened my mind to new experiences and experimentation, and I'm still guided by that. He never stood still – he kept on evolving and finding inspiration in unexpected places. In 1979 he went to Kingston, Jamaica, and recorded his album *Aux armes et cætera* with some of the most famous reggae musicians around. The title track was a reggae adaptation of the French national anthem, 'La Marseillaise', which provoked an outcry among the far right in France. He received death threats, bomb warnings and demands to strip him of his citizenship. French paratroopers even turned up to his gig in Strasbourg to voice their anger. They thought it was a disgrace that he would dishonour France in this way, in the city where 'La Marseillaise' was actually written. But Serge was undaunted and took to the stage alone. He sang an a cappella version of the song and won over the crowd. The protesting paratroopers ended up singing along!

Serge and the Sex Pistols were both outraging the establishment each side of the Channel and I loved them for it. Serge's version of the national anthem literally had people up in arms, and the Sex Pistols' 'God Save the Queen', released during the Queen's Silver Jubilee of 1977, was banned from being played by the BBC and from sale in major retailers.

Members of the band were even attacked by people armed with knives and iron bars.

To the Brits, the behaviour of the Sex Pistols was probably more shocking than Serge Gainsbourg's was to the French though, because their brazen disrespect went against the grain of how the Brits typically behave – not wanting to shock or upset people. But it was the fashion of the punk movement that really got to the French because it was such a shock to a society that dressed so conservatively. Even in the eighties, fashion was still so elegant and classy, as it had been for generations. Punk was a threat to the commercial order of things in France because it democratised fashion. Anyone could make and embellish their clothes to get the look, and to young people with nothing in the bank, that was as accessible as it was appealing.

As France was getting more and more stale in the 1990s, Cool Britannia was making Britain the place everyone wanted to be. Music, film, art – it was all going on in the UK. I used to spend a lot of time in London galleries in the late nineties – Britain has the best museums and galleries in the world, by the way, and they're free, which is wonderful. In 1997, so many cultural changes were happening in Britain. That year was like a whirlwind. There was a new Labour government in 10 Downing Street. Britain even won the Eurovision Song Contest. Also in September, Charles Saatchi pulled together the work of forty-two artists working in Britain for the *Sensation* show. Everyone was talking about it. It was the now legendary exhibition with Damien Hirst's shark suspended in formaldehyde, Tracey Emin's tent featuring the names of everyone she'd slept with, and Chris Ofili's *The Holy Virgin Mary*. I saw it twice and was completely blown away both times. It was impossible to be indifferent when presented with something like that – and I'd never seen a crowd in an art gallery so animated about what they were witnessing. For me, it was the most incredible exhibition I'd ever seen because it was so experimental, provocative and forward-thinking. I think art has to be ahead of its time – though, inevitably, some people find it difficult to adapt to it, or feel like they're being attacked. I felt so excited and privileged that I got to witness such a big moment. It just reinforced the sense that I was living in a place that was so alive with possibility.

British designers were making the clothes that everyone was talking about. It felt like even the French conceded that if they couldn't beat the

Brits they'd join them. So, when Ozwald Boateng made history by becoming the first tailor to stage a catwalk show at the 1994 Paris Fashion Week, renowned French fashion house Givenchy offered him a job – to 'reinvent the French gentleman'. France needed an injection of excitement and change, but to turn to a Brit for help was something that hadn't been done before, at least publicly. It was an acknowledgement that the Brits had style. And part of the reason for that was because Britain was embracing its diversity. Ozwald Boateng is the son of Ghanaian immigrants, who'd emigrated to the UK in the 1950s. He got his first suit when he was eight – a purple mohair number – and learned how to design and make clothes on his mother's old sewing machine. When it came to finding his own style, he managed to respect traditional tailoring while looking to the future. That was exactly what Savile Row needed to stay relevant. Ozwald was a pioneer and a visionary and I got to know him a bit when I was the maître d' at the restaurant Sartoria, on Savile Row, where Ozwald was a charming and always impeccably dressed regular. For me, Ozwald's success represented one of many threads in the cultural tapestry of Britain that made it such an exciting place to be. Like I say, that's because

Britain had this ability and openness to draw influences from many different places and cultures and proudly incorporate them into its story.

As a working-class woman, Vivienne Westwood recognised that the odds were against her succeeding in fashion. When she and Malcolm McLaren opened their SEX boutique on London's King's Road in 1971, it was seen by many as utterly scandalous. But it became the promised land to the punks. Before long, she was exhibiting in Paris. Her first and most famous catwalk show, 'Pirates', was inspired by the fashionable Parisian Incroyables after the French Revolution – the same group who had inspired Beau Brummell's style. And then Beau Brummell created his own aesthetic and became the most stylish person on the Continent, inspiring the French. The British and French are always learning from and influencing each other. Cultural exchange has been part of our histories and there have been periods of great collaboration, even if we don't always acknowledge it. I remember the French being so proud of the Concorde programme. At the time, though, no one in France mentioned that it was a collaboration with the Brits. To us, it was a French plane. While for the Brits, even though the 'e' spelling was a distant (and possibly irritating) reminder of French involvement, it was still seen as a British triumph. Both sides of the Channel chose not to honour the partnership at the time, but without each other, it never would have been possible!

As for my own style, after flirting with heavy metal in my teens, I went through a kind of summer-of-love hippy phase. We're talking flared trousers and a floral shirt, flowery bracelets and chains around my neck. When I was at catering college in Souillac, I worked in restaurants in the evenings and at weekends so I was able to save up for the thing I wanted most in the world at that point: a Perfecto biker jacket, not far off the John Travolta look in *Grease*. It cost an absolute fortune at the time but I loved that look.

La Tante Claire being such a high-end restaurant, I had to wear a uniform with a bow tie. You needed to look absolutely immaculate all the time for the customers because you were the embodiment of the brand. When you climb up the ranks in hospitality, though, eventually you end up wearing a suit. And then you've got a bit of choice with the kind of colours, shapes and styles you go for. For my next job interview, I went to a proper shop to try a pin-stripe suit. I chose one with really thick white lines. I thought it was so cool. I didn't take it off when

I bought it, I wore it out of the shop and hailed a black cab. I didn't even have anywhere to go, but I didn't care. I felt like a million dollars!

Twenty years ago, hospitality was still very traditional as an industry so I tended to wear quite muted colours at work. But around the time *First Dates* came up, I wanted to shake things up. The era of the French-racing-blue suit (or a royal-blue suit as Brits would say) had started. I never looked back. That year, I stopped wearing ties and I set myself free. I felt much more able to be creative and imaginative.

I know this might come as a shock to some, but I'm not always in suits. I still like to look the part, though, with clothes that fit, are cut well and make me feel confident. But obviously, you can't always be dapper and looking like you've won a BAFTA. If I'm out gardening, you definitely won't find me on the front cover of *Vogue*!

Fruitcake and I love to go out and dress for the occasion. She heads upstairs and then ten minutes later she comes down looking like a princess. It turns out that the effortlessly elegant, stylish and beautiful Frenchwoman I've been searching for my whole life was here, in south-east London! And she's even better, because she curated the ensemble and is proud of the fact that it hasn't cost the earth. She knows how to look good on a budget. The trouble is, when she comes downstairs, I look at what I've thrown on and realise I need to seriously up my game!

I'm fifty-two years old but I feel young and I'm full of energy, and I like my clothes to reflect that. Only recently I bought some Air Jordans because they look and feel great, and I enjoy the fact that anyone my kids' age does a double-take when they see them. It's a combination of *Who does this guy think he is?* and a slightly begrudging admission that *Actually they do look pretty good!* I know I'm perceived to be a stylish man, so sometimes I like to have some fun with that. I posted a video of me in my kitchen dancing to Beyoncé and I'm wearing white socks with my sandals. I know it's the ultimate no-no for Brits. A fatal fashion faux pas outside the house. But I'm inside my house! I like that some people will laugh with me and some at me. I enjoy taking the piss out of myself and that sense of humour is something unique to Brits. They do it with style and a smile. When I'm at home with my friends, I'm not trying to impress anybody. I'm relaxed and so my clothes match that. I want to have fun the way I am and I don't want to put any filters on. What you see is me.

6

'British Wine is Undrinkable'

Debunking the French myth that British wine is undrinkable would be a very short chapter if only you could join me here at home sipping a glass of Hambledon Première Cuvée English sparkling wine. It's pure pleasure in a bottle!

I first drank wine in my early teens. It was a permanent fixture of home life in Limoges – there was always a bottle of wine on the table for lunch and dinner. And there'd always be a sense of anticipation and excitement. We'd discuss where it was from and what kind of flavour profile it might have. Then, pop! You start nosing it and you talk some more about it. Then you drink it and you can't help but discuss what you're tasting because it's oxygenating and the flavour profile is changing. It's amazing knowing that wine is evolving in front of your eyes and on your palate. The whole experience became such a pleasurable ritual, each and every time.

For me, wine is about delighting the senses. We make sense of life through what we see, smell, taste and touch and wine is very much part of that. Around 50 per cent of the pleasure of wine arrives through your nose and once you learn to detect flavours and appreciate the different layers, you realise how much there is going on in a glass of wine. It has the power to evoke memories and take you on a sensual journey. In short, it opens up a completely new world.

Wine still had an association with the rich and the famous even into the 1980s but it shouldn't be that way – we all have the same senses, so we can all appreciate wine. That's the message I tried to distil in my book *Wine Uncorked*, demystifying wine and making it accessible for everyone by showing how easy wine is to understand and take pleasure in. That was only published in 2022, and the number of awards that British wines have picked up since then is staggering.

I'm a massive fan of British wines and sparkling ones in particular. They just get better and better. At the 2023 International Wine Challenge (IWC), English sparkling wines were second in the medal table behind France. Two golds went to Kent's beautiful Chapel Down winery, which makes me proud, being a Kent local. Sussex also put in a fantastic showing, with Rathfinny Estate, Busi Jacobsohn and Wiston Estate all winning golds. Hampshire did even better, winning the most golds of any English county and picking up the English Sparkling Trophy for Hattingley Valley's Blanc de Blancs 2014. Likewise, at the International

Wine & Spirit Competition, where an international panel of experts blind-taste thousands of wines, two Hampshire sparklers picked up gold medals: Hattingley Valley Wines Classic Reserve Brut NV and RAIMES English Sparkling Classic Brut 2018. Britain's in the Premier League of sparkling wine producers now.

The truth is that all these awards don't come as much of a surprise any more – the quality of English sparkling wines is well known. But what isn't that well known is how much still wines have progressed, and not just in southern England. England and Wales won twenty-four IWC medals for still wines in 2023, and they were awarded to producers across nineteen regions, including emerging winemakers from Staffordshire, Shropshire and Cornwall. This would have been completely unthinkable even ten years ago. Not bad for a newcomer.

Only, Britain isn't exactly a newcomer. Britain started making wine around thirty years after the Roman invasion in AD 43 when Europe was experiencing higher than normal temperatures and periods of low rainfall. Fast-forward to William the Conqueror's spectacularly detailed Domesday Book of 1085–6 and we know that there were forty-two vineyards in England. Only twelve of them were attached to monasteries, to produce communion wine, so the other thirty were commercial vineyards, recently planted by England's new rulers. But the Norman attempt to kick-start a wine industry here didn't work. After 1150, Brits were far keener on fine wines imported from Bordeaux and La Rochelle. And that put a cork in British winemaking.

British wine production only really started again 800 years later, in the 1950s, with the emergence of Hambledon, now the oldest commercial vineyard in the country. In the 1960s and 70s, vineyards began to pop up in the south of England. Stephen Spurrier, a British wine merchant, opened a little wine shop in Paris that allowed customers to taste wines before they bought them. He became well known for setting up France's first private wine school, the Académie du Vin, as well as for serving English sparkling wine at a reception at Versailles to President Georges Pompidou and Queen Elizabeth II in 1972. But he became famous all over the wine world in 1976 for the competition he organised with colleague Patricia Gallagher. They came up with an idea to pit Californian wine – the new kid on the block in the wine world – against the finest French wines. Spurrier invited nine influential wine experts from across France to blind-taste four top-quality white burgundies and four of the best red Bordeaux wines, alongside six Californian Chardonnays and six Californian reds. For the white wines, Chateau Montelena 1973 was the winner. From California! What's more, three of the Californian white wines were in the top five. For the reds, California only went and won the best red as well for Stag's Leap Wine Cellars 1973. The event went down in history as the Judgement of Paris. It was a game-changer for New World wines.

In 2016, I was part of a blind-tasting competition organised by *Noble Rot* magazine. There were thirteen of us, including wine expert Jancis Robinson, chef Stephen Harris, Kate Spicer from the *Sunday Times*, and sommeliers Xavier Rousset and Raphael Rodriguez. The tasting featured twelve wines and (not that we knew this at the time) eight were champagnes, and four were English sparkling wines. The winner was ... Hambledon Classic Cuvée NV. In second place was another English sparkling wine: Nyetimber Classic Cuvée Brut 2010. I was delighted! Even the French tasters had to acknowledge it was 'a fair cop' as Brits would say.

The result wasn't a one-off – the same year, wine writer Matthew Jukes conducted a blind-taste test hosted by the Wine and Spirit Trade Association in Paris. There were three categories: Chardonnay-based, rosé and blends, and each test was a kind of shoot-out. Nyetimber 2009 Blanc de Blancs was preferred to NV Billecart-Salmon Grand Cru Blanc de Blancs by nine of the panel of fourteen. Thirteen of them believed the English wine was actually French. In the rosé head-to-head, the 2011 Gusbourne Rosé was preferred by nine of the panel over the NV Ayala Rosé Majeur Champagne. Seven of the panel believed the English rosé was French. In the blends category, the judges couldn't split the English Ridgeview 2009 and the NV Jacquesson Cuvée no. 738, and, again, half the panel thought the English wine was French. This was another coup for the Brits but no one seemed to be listening!

I wondered about the Judgement of Paris while I continued sipping my lovely glass of Hambledon Première Cuvée Brut NV at home. It's a blend of the three traditional champagne varieties, made from grapes grown in very similar soils to that of the best crus of Champagne. It made me contemplate what the result might be if there was a Judgement of London, exactly fifty years later, pitting English sparkling wine against the best sparkling wines around the world in a blind tasting. We've got nothing to lose and, in a blind tasting, you never know what's going to happen. A lot of people love champagne because of the label and what buying champagne says about their own social status. Even the brand of champagne you choose reveals something about you. If you choose Krug, for example, you're posh (and rich)! Champagne is all about perception. But when you cover the label and no one can see the name, then suddenly it's just about what's in the bottle and how your palate reacts. A big 'Judgement of London' event is the kind of major PR coup that would bring the Brits into the Premier League with the French, the Italians and the Spanish. If the best British sparkling wines, like Hambledon, Nyetimber, Balfour and Chapel Down, came out on top, which they could, I think it would change everything. It would change the perception. It would also help establish the brands across the world.

Britain's already done it with cider, which has a proud history going back hundreds of years. There's no question that Britain produces the best cider in the world. Or should I say 'cyder', as they call it at the Newt, the stunning Somerset hotel I visited with my friend Michel Roux Jr. The Newt has sixty-five acres of orchards and they make their own cyder.

They spell it that way to preserve an old tradition, with the 'y' indicating superior strength and quality. I can't say 'cider' without speaking in a West Country accent – I think you have to. Somerset is the apple orchard *par excellence* of England and cider is naturally the county's favourite tipple. Back in 1698, when Hadspen House – the main building comprising the Newt – was being built, people in England drank a lot of cider. It was much safer than water in those days, and everyone drank it, including the kids – even at breakfast!

The cyders at the Newt are so good that they suggest them as food pairings for their menu, just like you would do with wines. They are all produced with 100 per cent apple juice using a state-of-the-art cyder press and cyder cellar and advanced cold-press techniques. There was a single varietal made with Dabinett apples that Michel and I enjoyed with the most delicious fresh oysters. It was slightly smoky, with notes of citrus and apple orchard. On the palate, it was dry, elegant, fruity and moreish with a smooth finish. It was perfect with the shellfish. I love British oysters. They're fat, juicy and creamy – just the way I like them. After lunch, I wandered around the gardens at the Newt and saw their beautiful orchards. I couldn't help but draw a parallel with expert winemaking because the same care, attention to detail, proud heritage and sprinkling of magic was all on show.

The trouble is, British winemaking just doesn't have the same reach yet. Everyone in Britain and beyond knows Somerset cider/cyder is the best in the business. But at the moment, not enough British consumers know and recognise British wine, let alone consumers beyond Britain. Some restaurants and bars feature British sparkling wines but there aren't nearly enough selling it by the glass. That's because they'll make a loss if they don't sell enough of it. English sparkling wines still aren't readily available in the supermarket. Suppliers might have confidence in the quality of the product but they don't have confidence in the consumer's perception of the quality of the product. Maybe that will happen over time, but I think something monumental needs to happen to shake things up. The world needs to know how good British wine is!

Once the world is talking about it, that's when you make the big long-term investment in marketing and PR to maximise brand awareness. Big brands like Coca-Cola and Pepsi have never stopped advertising and innovating. Marketing was such a big factor in the rise of champagne, establishing the drink's association with celebration, success, sophistication and luxury. Everything about champagne has been well crafted. They aren't champagne brands – they're champagne 'houses'. Immediately, you get the sense of prestige, heritage and nobility. You're already storytelling. And that story might include an image of a vineyard in a picturesque landscape, where you'll find a wise old artisan lovingly tending a vine, having perfected his craft over a lifetime. Everything's done by hand as it has been for generations, using ancient techniques. There's also the message of exclusivity and scarcity – champagne can only be made in Champagne, and there are strict regulations to ensure quality. Then you've got the sponsorship of high-profile events, fashion shows, and celebrity endorsements and collaborations, like Karl Lagerfeld designing limited-edition Dom Pérignon bottles, which furthers the reach of the brand.

I'm not saying that Brits have to emulate champagne but it would be great to create their own history and legacy. But let's not get carried away, as demonstrated by the swiftly abandoned idea to call English sparkling wine 'Britagne'. Brits need to plough their own furrow, but they're in a strong position to start from. While Brits are relative newcomers to the party, it means they can learn exactly how other markets have achieved success and draw inspiration from them.

Quality-wise, British wines are only going to keep getting better, and that makes me very happy. Part of that's down to the experience that growers are gaining about which grapes to use and the landscape and conditions, but there's also something else contributing towards that: climate change. Although this is terrible news, it's not so bad for the future of British wine. Since the 1980s, the grape-growing season has seen an increase of over 1°C in southern and south-eastern England. In the past five years (2018–23), the total amount of land under vine in England and Wales has surged by 74 per cent. According to WineGB, there are 943 vineyards in Great Britain as at 2023, and official government figures reveal that viticulture is the fastest growing agricultural sector in the UK. Brits might soon be beating the French at their own game!

Chardonnay is the most planted grape variety in the UK, followed closely by Pinot Noir, then Pinot Meunier. But Bacchus, named after the god of wine, is now the fourth-most planted variety here. And that shows how things are changing because Bacchus is mainly used to make still wine. Thank

God the authorities changed the name of the grape to Bacchus, because when it was created in Germany in 1933 (by crossing Sylvaner, Riesling and Müller-Thurgau grapes), it was named 'Geilweilerhof 32-29-133'. The plan back then was to grow an early ripening grape with a fruity bouquet and high sugar content, which would work well in southern Germany. The conditions in parts of the UK are now more similar to southern Germany, so Bacchus can thrive here. Grapes like Sauvignon Blanc, Sémillon and Riesling may all start to flourish as well. Investors in winemaking have got wise to the fact that, in Britain, they're going to benefit from a steady income for years to come. Plus, it becomes an even smarter long-term investment because the vines become better as they age (don't we all).

As votes of confidence go in British vineyards, the French have already delivered one. Pierre-Emmanuel Taittinger (no guesses which champagne house he runs) is an Anglophile, like me. He made headlines in 2019 by admitting in an interview for *Le Figaro* that the English had invented champagne, albeit accidentally. The story goes that still red and white wines, made by Benedictine monks from Champagne, were shipped across the English Channel, but left for a time at the docks in London. That triggered a second fermentation, which added the bubbles. 'They created champagne,' Pierre-Emmanuel said, to the delight of British newspapers. Four years earlier, he had joined forces with UK partner Hatch Mansfield to set up Domaine Evremond. They planted thirty hectares of Chardonnay, Pinot Noir and Pinot Meunier vines near the village of Chilham in Kent in 2017 and their first sparkling wine is due to appear late in 2024. The Entente Cordiale is back in business!

This is all really exciting stuff but I'm not sure anyone knows what they're going to put on the label, because the classification system in the UK is a bit of a mess. At the moment, the top category of wine in the UK (and the EU) is PDO (protected designation of origin), which is the most closely monitored production-wise. PDO wines have to be made entirely from grapes grown within the country marked on the label. The next tier down is PGI (protected geographical indication), which must be labelled 'English Regional Wine' or 'Welsh Regional Wine' and feature 85 per cent of grapes made from the country on the label. But, in the post-Brexit landscape, PDO and PGI are only recognised in the UK and haven't yet been registered with the EU's separate GI (geographical indications) system.

And that's not doing a lot to spread the word abroad.

When Sussex was awarded a PDO in July 2022, which means Sussex wine has the same legal status as Stilton cheese and Jersey Royal potatoes, it made the headlines. While the PDO does introduce standards that guarantee certain levels of quality and consistency, like needing to use the 'traditional method' (the method used to produce champagne), requiring grapes to be harvested by hand and the formation of a tasting panel (to exclude poorer quality wine), there are some big problems with it. Awarding a PDO like this basically implements a two-tier system, elevating one region above the others. What about Kent and Hampshire, for example, which produce some of the best British wines and have almost identical soils and climates?

I think it would have been better to establish a unified category for English sparkling wine to help form an identity. Within that category, you could have separate classifications based on the different regions. Then you could have a sub-classification for the towns and villages within those regions. At the moment in the UK, it's all quite confusing. We need a proper framework to set the minimum standards and separate the good wines from the table wines. It's long overdue. Clarity is one of the most important things about wine. You need to know what you're looking at and what you're getting. It needs to do what it says on the tin. Get that right, and everyone around the world can start to see it for what it is.

In the past, the wine world has been a little reluctant to embrace emerging talent. As my parents have taught me well, the establishment's always resistant to a threat to the status quo! But we have to shake things up from time to time, to try new things, learn and grow.

Back in the 1990s, there were so few female sommeliers in restaurants but thankfully things began to change when wine professional Joëlle Marti arrived in London. Joëlle Marti and I go way back, all the way to catering college nearly thirty-five years ago in Souillac. We both had a love for the UK; I left France for London in 1992 and Joëlle made the same move a few years later. Before then, she took a job in Australia – a smart move because it meant her knowledge of New World wines became really impressive. In fact, she became a big advocate of the New World, which isn't that common for wine professionals from France. Isn't that just absurd?

London was the place to be though, and she shook up the restaurant scene in 1996 by becoming the head sommelier at Conran's La Pont de la Tour. She was the first female head sommelier in London. She drew upon her knowledge and experience to teach the professionals she trained up about the Old World and the New – the best of both worlds. Joëlle and I are still good friends, and we share a special history, being raised and trained in the same part of France, but falling in love with the UK and choosing to spend our lives here.

When I started my career in London, nearly all of the sommeliers in restaurants were French, plus a few Italians and Spaniards. It's a very different picture now, with sommeliers of all different nationalities. I think Brits are much more into wine now, and that's reflected in the number of British wine directors, buyers, vineyard owners, wine experts and sommeliers.

When Fruitcake and I went down to Cornwall a few years ago, we went for dinner at Paul Ainsworth at No. 6 and Elly Owen was the head sommelier. She knows everything there is to know about wine and has that unique gift to connect with people in such an engaging, kind, honest way. Fruitcake and I were so pleased that she was awarded Sommelier of the Year in 2020. 'Not bad for a woman from Cornwall,' Elly said at the awards. She's a proud advocate of British wines. And if ever there was an ambassador for the hospitality business, she'd be the one.

As for the myth about British wines being undrinkable, just sit down with a glass of Nyetimber, Hambledon or Balfour, or a glass of Chapel Down, with its golden-coloured sparkling wine that reminds me of Kent's stunning wheat fields when they're ripe for harvesting. You'll be knocked out.

7

'British Food is Bland and Boring'

Two months after I started work at La Tante Claire, the restaurant was awarded a third Michelin star. Winning three Michelin stars is seen by many in the hospitality industry as the highest professional accolade and it was an incredible moment to be even a little part of that. I came to the UK wanting to work in the Premier League of restaurants, alongside the very best in the business. Suddenly, I was there!

No other restaurant in London had three Michelin stars. If you wanted a career in hospitality at that time, you couldn't work anywhere more stylish, more professional, more challenging or more rewarding than La Tante Claire. It was a wonderful feeling knowing that right then, there was no better team in the capital – not even at the Roux brothers' legendary Le Gavroche (named after the urchin character Gavroche in Victor Hugo's *Les Misérables*), a groundbreaking restaurant in the history of British gastronomy. Master chef Bernard Loiseau, who I met when I was working at Le Gavroche a couple of years later, used to talk about *le top du top*. The cream of the crop. At La Tante Claire, that was us. But it's one thing to win three Michelin stars; it's another thing holding on to them. When I found out that we had retained that third star the following year, it felt even better because

I was helping maintain that success. It confirmed our status as a truly elite team of professionals.

From my very first day in the restaurant, I lived and breathed hospitality. I was so excited to put into practice all the things I'd learned at catering college and in the places I'd worked. It was the start of my quest for excellence. You see, I don't do anything by halves. I was completely focused on creating memorable experiences and delighting our customers every day. That's all I wanted: to provide the greatest service imaginable and serve the greatest food. I loved that service was about the spirit of generosity, finding a way to engage and connect with people and deliver something exceptional every single time. We were always attentive and always smiling. Nothing was too much trouble. Whatever our customers wanted, we'd give to them. Everything would appear like it was effortless and easy because that's what we'd striven to create. For our diners, we took great pride in conjuring a fairy-tale world for each meal. Our regulars adored the food and the service and we loved that it gave them a lot of pleasure. They'd arrive for lunch at 12.30 p.m. and spend the next few hours talking, eating, drinking and laughing. By 5 p.m., they were on to the cheese. Come 6 p.m., they were enjoying brandies and coffees. It was a golden age of hospitality back then. Lunch really was an all-day affair!

I spent just over a year at La Tante Claire. You have to do your time in a restaurant, and for me, that was a minimum of a year. Some people come and go after a few months, but I don't think you can learn everything you need to and assimilate in less than twelve months. If you want to further your career and make the most of your training, you need to do your time everywhere you go. My plan was to work in a different restaurant to broaden my experience and learn new skills, but everything had to be put on hold: I got the phone call I knew would come one day – the call-up for military service.

I didn't want to go at all, but I had no choice – military service was still compulsory in France until 1996. So, I went from loving living in London, an exciting, dynamic new city where I was finding my feet, to a grey block of flats on the outskirts of Paris. I was stationed at Balard, the headquarters of the French Air Force during the week, but I returned to London almost every weekend I could on the ferry. I couldn't wait to be back.

A year later, when I was released from military service, I was desperate to pick up where I'd left off.

And there was only one place I wanted to go: Le Gavroche. So I approached them to ask them for a job. I didn't need to send a CV – I just asked my former manager at La Tante Claire to talk to his counterpart at Le Gavroche, and I was hired the next day. No interview, nothing. Hospitality is an incestuous industry and that was how you got jobs back then. You built up your reputation, showed people that you were reliable, true and trustworthy, and that spoke for itself. I was making a name for myself and could have worked anywhere, but I wanted to work at Le Gavroche. It was iconic, full every day, and everyone was talking about it. It was *the* place to work.

I know it might seem odd to leave a restaurant at the height of its success like La Tante Claire, but Le Gavroche was an institution – the original. The first restaurant in the UK to get a Michelin star. Another *top du top*, if you like. The chef-patron at La Tante Claire was Pierre Koffmann, who started at Le Gavroche in London as a twenty-two-year-old before becoming head chef at the Roux brothers' Waterside Inn in Berkshire two years later. La Tante Claire's success was built on their shoulders. As was the direction of British gastronomy from 1967.

Albert Roux and his younger brother Michel both trained as pastry chefs in Paris before going on to work together at the British Embassy near the Avenue des Champs-Élysées. Soon after Albert moved to England, Michel followed him. In 1967, they gathered together all of their savings, borrowed money from the bank and opened Le Gavroche in Sloane Square. They were on a mission to bring French cooking to the UK. Michel made his feelings about British cuisine back then very clear. 'The food was so awful,' he told the *Guardian*'s Rachel Cooke in 2004. In Michel's memoir *Life is a Menu*, he recalled seeing someone happily eating peas and white bread through the window of Maison Lyons Corner House in Marble Arch, and wrote: 'Like a witness to a terrible atrocity, I told myself I had to put this out of my mind as quickly as possible.' Ouch.

Le Gavroche was a complete game-changer. Before then, except for a couple of chains like Lyons, restaurants in the UK were basically attached to expensive hotels visited by the rich and famous. One of the Roux brothers' great achievements was to popularise the stand-alone restaurant.

I started at Le Gavroche around a year after Albert's son Michel Roux Jr had taken over the kitchen. I really liked Michel as soon as I met him because he was very kind and I could tell he had a good heart. Michel spoke French fluently with a perfect French accent but he could also speak English fluently with an English accent, which just wasn't fair! He was, and still is, incredibly hard-working. He was always the first in and the last out. I admired him, but the reason why we've remained in contact and stayed friends is because he's reliable, trustworthy and good-natured.

I remember thinking it must be hard for Michel Jr, being in his early thirties taking over such a famous kitchen from Albert, who had such a formidable reputation. One day, not long after I'd started at Le Gavroche, I asked him: 'Chef, it must be hard for you to take over your dad's kitchen – how do you feel about it?' He looked at me for a few seconds deep in thought, but didn't say anything. It told me a lot about what it must have been like. A few chefs have had to fill shoes that large. But I can't remember any chefs who had to fill shoes that large that were owned by their father. That's a tough gig.

Albert and Michel Sr ensured that Le Gavroche was profitable from day one, which as anyone in the restaurant business will know is a very rare thing. They knew how to run a kitchen and how to run the hospitality side of things, but they also had a well-thought-out strategy: they cut out the middlemen by going direct to farmers and suppliers to source their produce. I found out more about this on a memorable night in the English countryside at Albert's house in the late 1990s.

I got to know Albert because he'd often appear at Le Gavroche. And then one day, he asked me to help look after his guests at the Christmas party he held at his house in the country. Albert absolutely loved entertaining, and his festive dinners were legendary. He always made sure they were a feast for the senses with beautiful food and amazing wines. He'd ask a couple of chefs from Le Gavroche to do the cooking and a young waiter to serve the twenty or so guests he'd invited, which included some of the most famous chefs in the world.

The year I went, the one and only chef Paul Bocuse (the man that trained the Roux brothers) was there. The whole group went out hunting during the day, and that evening Irish stew was on the menu for the main course. Paul Bocuse looked at the stew, then looked at Albert and said: 'Albert – that is cooking!' and he started to clap loudly just by himself. It was proper food porn to these guys. I noticed that he had an Opinel, the beautiful wooden-handled pocket knife that you can use for pretty much everything. It's a French classic. We got chatting and Paul told me he'd send me one. He even took down my address. I didn't think he'd actually follow through with it though, so when a package arrived through my door from Paul Bocuse a few weeks later, I was stunned. Alas, there was no Opinel, but I treasured what he did send: a few words of wisdom and one of his famous ties. I was so proud of that tie!

Back to the Christmas dinner. The event went on well into the night, so I stayed over and Albert drove me back home the next day in his car. I couldn't help but notice a strange-looking shape in the boot. 'It's a whole lamb, Fred. Picked it up today!' he said, beaming. He'd done this a hundred times, but still his joy was like a kid on Christmas morning.

He said they'd keep the fillet and the shoulder for Le Gavroche and all the other parts would go to other restaurants or the butcher's shop they owned. Albert was at least sixty years old at the time and he absolutely loved sourcing meat and produce directly from farmers and distributing it himself to his restaurants. It's no wonder the Roux brothers were so successful, when they did things like that. They were the complete package, both as chefs and restaurateurs, because it wasn't just about cooking for them – it was about understanding farming, agriculture, seasons and produce. They also mastered the art of establishing long-term relationships with farmers and suppliers. And they went about their work with passion and excitement which was infectious to everyone around them. But maybe most importantly, they felt a sense of responsibility to inspire the next generation. And that's how you create a movement. It's not just about what *you* do – it's about the people you bring with you. That's the legacy the Roux brothers left to gastronomy in the UK.

I love history. It adds colour and context and makes you see things in a different way. So I took a dive into the '*rosbifs*' stereotype that the French have been regurgitating about British food being bland and boring. I've discovered that the expression goes back to the early eighteenth century, when it was used just as a gastronomic term to describe the traditional British way of cooking beef. The Brits were proud of the quality of their beef and the way they cooked it. They still are! In 1731, Henry Fielding even wrote the ballad 'The Roast Beef of Old England' for his play *The Grub Street Opera*. The song soon became a symbol of national pride, and for a time it was a cultural tradition for theatre audiences to sing it before a new play was performed in London. It also became the anthem of beefsteak clubs in British cities and was sung by the Royal Navy before formal mess dinners.

But the song struck a different note in the climate of fear of a French invasion in the late eighteenth century, which hardened the British establishment against their neighbours across the water. Napoleon had conquered most of Central Europe and made no secret of his plans, famously saying: 'I want only for a favourable wind to plant the Imperial Eagle on the Tower of London.' Suddenly 'The Roast Beef of Old England' wasn't just about celebrating the best of British. It was about differentiating *us* from *them*.

And so the claim arose that British meat was better than the meat in France. As did the claims that British meat could just be enjoyed simply cooked, unlike in France, where lower-quality meat needed to be disguised with elaborate sauces. The message was that honest, hearty British beef makes you strong. British cattle became a metaphor for strength and power, and landowners went to great lengths to rear gigantic cattle so as to symbolise superiority – a PR stunt that massively backfired though, because the meat became really fatty. At the same time, the way the French were perceived, *concealing their lower-quality meat with clever sauces*, morphed into insults about national characteristics. So the French became tricksters, untrustworthy and deceitful. Always up to something!

We're not exactly sure when '*rosbifs*' became an insulting term for the Brits, but we know that in 1734, just three years after *The Grub Street Opera* was first performed, a French play called *The Frenchman in London* opened in the West End featuring a rude, coarse and unfashionable English character called Jack Roastbeef, so perhaps it was around then. Britain was increasingly perceived by the French as backward, uncivilised and unpleasant around this time. And these characteristics were exaggerated in popular cartoons to poke fun at or insult the Brits during a period of great rivalry between the two nations. When the rivalry spilled over onto the battlefield, these depictions were amplified even further.

In fact, despite the stereotypes, the vast majority of British and French people ate very similar things. The diet basically featured grains, bread, root vegetables and dairy products, and if they had any meat at all, it was usually pork. It was a different matter among the elite, though. While the two countries weren't fighting each other, French cuisine became very fashionable in Britain. French chefs had developed an international reputation for creating exciting, experimental and elaborate food, so anyone who was anyone had a French cook. It was a status symbol and a way of showing off.

One of the pioneers was Antonin Carême, the founder of French gastronomy and the world's first 'celebrity' chef. His ideas took root in post-revolutionary France where restaurants began to flourish, staffed by the former cooks of executed and exiled aristocrats. Carême published best-selling cookbooks, with step-by-step instructions, which made his techniques accessible. Legendary chef Auguste Escoffier modernised and streamlined Carême's methods and fused them with his own ideas. He became known as 'the king of chefs and the chef of kings', but it wasn't in France that he forged his reputation. It was actually in London, at the Savoy between 1890 and 1898, and the Carlton from 1899. These were the places that wealthy folks went to have French haute cuisine in the UK. In the 1920s, the chef and restaurateur Xavier Marcel Boulestin popularised simple French cooking in

Britain, and in the 1930s, French-inspired yet recognisably British dishes began to appear, but then World War II broke out and everything changed.

In the depressing post-war landscape with rationing still going on, it's easy to see why Elizabeth David's first cookbook, *A Book of Mediterranean Food*, was such a hit in 1950. She presented what must have sounded like paradise – sunny climes, plentiful food, colourful landscapes and, most importantly, optimism for a happier future – to a British public who'd been starved of it all. Fanny Cradock became Britain's first TV cook and introduced audiences to new recipes and techniques. She gave cooking a sprinkling of glamour, appearing in an evening dress and a pearl necklace. Like Elizabeth David, though, Fanny Cradock focused on opening British eyes to the idea of French and Mediterranean food at home. But if you wanted that kind of food in a restaurant in the UK, you weren't exactly spoiled for choice. Until two brothers from eastern France came along.

When they started up Le Gavroche in 1967, the Roux brothers had a long-term vision, attracting chefs and hospitality professionals from all over the world. Not only was Le Gavroche the first restaurant in the UK to win a Michelin star, it was also the first to earn three. It became a culinary institution, but it also effectively became an educational institution. The chefs and hospitality professionals the Roux brothers trained up became very good at what they did and many of them took the skills and ideas they'd seen and learned to other parts of the UK. In a professional sense, almost everyone who is working now in hospitality in the UK is a descendant of the Roux brothers. We're talking about renowned chefs like Marco Pierre White, Gordon Ramsay and Marcus Wareing. They're all part of a dynasty that goes back several generations to the unsung heroine of French cuisine, Eugénie 'la Mère' Brazier, who, in 1933, became the first chef to win six Michelin stars.

While the Roux brothers were beginning to inspire a new generation of chefs in the 1960s, the whole cultural landscape of Britain was rapidly changing. Migrants from Commonwealth nations brought their cooking with them and Brits began to realise that flavour explosions from all around the world were within their grasp. In 1970, *The Good Food Guide* wrote that 'London now has a richer variety of restaurants than any other city on Earth'.

In 1972, Albert and Michel opened their second venture in the UK – the Waterside Inn in Bray,

Berkshire. Le Gavroche-trained Pierre Koffmann was the first head chef. It won its first Michelin star in 1974, then its second in 1977, before Koffmann left to open La Tante Claire in Chelsea. Michel Roux Sr took the reins at the Waterside after that, eventually handing over to his son Alain.

Meanwhile, on British TV screens, Delia Smith came along to reassure everyone with her down-to-earth style and to help translate and explain foreign techniques. The 'Delia effect' became a problem because supermarkets ran out of ingredients and utensils the day after one of her shows aired. The UK was becoming alive to new tastes and novel influences, but 'British cooking' was scarcely getting a mention, let alone a definition. That would only change in the 1980s, with a new crop of young British chefs.

This new generation of chefs identified the importance of seasonality and provenance. They helped us see how much incredible produce we had on these shores – we just had to go out and look for it. And this inspired original creations in the kitchen. British chefs were no longer imitating the cuisine of other countries; they were finding their own feet. With all this developing over the decades, the early 1990s became an incredible time to work in hospitality in the UK. When I started at Le Gavroche in 1995, I felt honoured to be connected to such an incredible dynasty including Paul Bocuse and 'la Mère' Brazier. Le Gavroche was also just such an exciting place to be, surrounded by young chefs and waiting staff from so many different countries and educational backgrounds. It felt like whenever I went into the restaurant, I was travelling the world. Here, all of us waiting staff were, in London, speaking English together. I loved how much of a melting pot Britain was.

In the mid-1990s, it was a Brit who took the baton from the Roux brothers and ran with it, and his name was Terence Conran. He specialised in turning unloved or faded buildings into sleek, modern and dynamic restaurants. He transformed whole areas of London, like Shad Thames, in the late 1980s and early 1990s. Conran became known for his large restaurants – Quaglino's was serving over 300 covers in an evening and Mezzo could handle 1,000 a day. That was pretty much unheard of in the UK hospitality scene at the time.

In the late 1990s, Conran took over what used to be the iconic 1920s Bluebird garage on the King's Road in Chelsea and turned it into the 'Bluebird

Gastrodome'. After leaving Le Gavroche, I worked for a time in contract catering for one of the big banks in the City, but it wasn't for me. It was quite formulaic and repetitive and the interaction with the guests was very limited. I look back on the experience as a really useful learning exercise that broadened my knowledge about another side of the hospitality industry, and it helped me realise what I wanted. The whole philosophy of what the new restaurant Bluebird was offering sounded like the polar opposite to the not-seen and not-heard service I'd provided in contract catering. It seemed like a place in which waiters could really express themselves and engage with the guests. 'We have personalities coming into the restaurant. We want personalities to serve them,' Craig, the assistant general manager, told me. *Sign me up*, I thought.

With its floor-to-ceiling windows, Bluebird was so light, bright and full of colour. Everyone who worked there seemed full of *joie de vivre*. Like Le Gavroche had been, Bluebird was the new place everyone wanted to be. The characters working there added a unique energy to the place. 'I bloody love this job. I dream about it!' Craig said in the first daily briefing to the staff after I joined. He was inspirational and confident and it brought out the best in us. It was a transformative moment because, until then, my experience in service had been one of respectful subservience to the customer. But here, we felt free to chat and laugh. Be the people we were. And that was easy with the customers, many of whom were around my age. Hospitality was metamorphosing in front of my eyes. I couldn't wait to get into work in the morning!

Terence had brought over talented chefs from Australia like John Torode and they made food sound so easy and simple. They'd talk about throwing in a few prawns, adding a bit of garlic, olive oil, tomato, chucking in some chilli and bang! It was the polar opposite to the French style, and I'd never seen anything like it. It felt completely revolutionary. And I loved it. So I learned how to work like an Australian. Their easy-going attitude towards life was a breath of fresh air. And that fed into the way they interacted with guests in the restaurant. They were just so relaxed, optimistic, friendly and informal. It was so different to the attention to detail, the perfectionism and rigour that I'd grown up with. But put those two cultures together, and you've got some cocktail.

Elsewhere, chefs like Gary Rhodes were shaking up the British food scene by reviving traditional

British fare like fishcakes and oxtail. Fergus Henderson, an architect by training, opened St John in 1994 on the site of a former smokehouse round the corner from Smithfield Market, a pretty unloved part of London at the time. The restaurant was a pared-down, whitewashed space with a short menu, mostly containing offal. It was a gamble, but it paid off, and a waste-not-want-not attitude evolved into a philosophy of nose-to-tail eating. The high-quality ingredients were on his doorstep from the historic meat market and some of his dishes, like bone marrow, became iconic. His stance on seasonal specialities was a revelation too. 'In Britain, if there is one thing we have, it is fantastic seasons ... Nature has always been writing this amazing menu for us – it's just that for a long while we forgot to listen to it,' he told *Observer Food Monthly*. St John became one of the best restaurants in the world.

By now, Britain's first rock star of a chef arrived on the stage: Marco Pierre White. When he was twenty, he moved from his native Yorkshire to start his classical training with the Rouxs at Le Gavroche. It wasn't unlike my own journey as a twenty-year-old with a one-way ferry ticket to London to work under a French maestro. Marco carried even less than me: a bag of clothes, a box of books and a little over £7 in his wallet! Maybe it was best he travelled light, because Marco was in a hurry to go places. And that's exactly what he did, working with the very best around, including Raymond Blanc and Nico Ladenis. In 1987, Marco opened his own restaurant – Harvey's – in Wandsworth, south London. That was an extraordinary year for British chefs, with Rowley Leigh opening Kensington Place and Terence Conran opening Bibendum. That was the year everything changed. That was the year that 'modern British cooking' properly started. Trailblazing British-born chefs were making the headlines.

In 1995, Marco Pierre White became the first British chef to gain three Michelin stars. But maybe the best of his achievements, to me anyway, was the next generation of British chefs he trained and inspired, including Gordon Ramsay. It was far from smooth sailing working with Marco Pierre White, as Gordon told Natalie Whittle from the *Financial Times* in 2017. 'Marco pushed us. Oh my God, that guy was ruthless, but fucking brilliantly ruthless, because he just wanted the best, and if you didn't give him the best, he'd let you know. The pay-off for me was what I was learning; I could tolerate the shit. You were on a path of utter perfection.'

Right about this time, Heston Blumenthal exploded onto the scene. A self-taught chef, he squirrelled away cash working for a time selling photocopiers and as a debt collector, and bought a run-down 450-year-old pub in the Berkshire village of Bray, just down the road from the Waterside Inn. He called it the Fat Duck. Heston pioneered what came to be known as 'molecular gastronomy', using scientific techniques, artistry, showmanship and fun to create a completely unique restaurant. His first paid job as a chef was in his own restaurant! And ten years later, the Fat Duck had three Michelin stars and was named the best restaurant in the world by the World's 50 Best Restaurants. Heston – a Brit – was the most exciting chef in the world.

By now, Gordon Ramsay had bought the former site of the first restaurant I worked at in London, La Tante Claire, and had turned it into Restaurant Gordon Ramsay. He'd already built a reputation for excellence in the kitchen and, like Marco Pierre White, his restaurants became a training ground for some of the most exciting British chefs around, like Marcus Wareing, Angela Hartnett and Mark Sargent. Gordon had taken a big gamble to set up Restaurant Gordon Ramsay, selling the flat he and his wife Tana owned in Wandsworth to raise the money. Just three years later, he was sitting pretty on three Michelin stars. He'd become a superstar.

When I met Gordon for the first time, it was clear from the handshake that this is a guy who needs to be in charge! What perhaps you don't see in Gordon until you know him is how attentive, generous and kind he is. The fact that he's super-competitive and combustible has presented some lovely and very easy opportunities to wind him up, which is a lot of fun for me and Gino when we're filming *Gordon, Gino and Fred's Road Trip*. Gino's a firecracker – he's little, he's loud and he burns very brightly. What people don't know about Gino is how precise, meticulous and professional he is. He's also a very loyal and reliable friend.

When the three of us are together, two things happen: Gordon is always right and Gino is never wrong! So I become a sort of diplomat. Actually, 'firefighter' might be a better word. Sometimes I can just about put out the fire; other times, I feel like I'm tackling an inferno with a glass of water and a drinking straw for a hose. We can just be having a quiet cappuccino together in a coffee shop, and then suddenly all hell breaks loose. It's like a tornado has just spontaneously appeared and I've no idea how it started or where it's headed.

What I've learned is that sometimes you've just got to let it blow itself out. Either Gordon or Gino (or both) gets upset, but once one of them has been upset for long enough, they realise how much they miss the friendship. So they get back in touch on the group chat with something like 'I miss you guys so much xxx' or send a bunch of heart emojis. I've never had friendships like this with anyone. 'Bromance' doesn't do it justice. It's a uniquely intense relationship. It's like we're in love – almost like we're three teenagers in a throuple. You just don't know what's going to happen. With everyone else in my life, I know, more or less, what's going on. With them, I've no bloody clue. There's nothing like it and I wouldn't change it for anything. It's totally bonkers.

Foraging took off in the UK in the mid-2000s. Young Danish chef René Redzepi had a lot to do with that, after he opened Noma in Copenhagen in 2003. Redzepi reinvented Nordic food, putting a focus on foraging (or 'treasure hunting', as he puts it), creativity, seasonality and locally sourced food. Noma was groundbreaking and the tremors resonated in the UK. One of the reasons foraging became such a big deal here was because we realised how much incredible wild food we have and not just in woodland, along the coast and in the countryside, but also in city centres. Chefs were rediscovering humble delicacies that have existed here for thousands of years, like marsh samphire, wild garlic, parasol mushrooms, sweet chestnuts, hazelnuts and sloes, and incorporating them into their menus.

The UK has some of the world's best oysters. The Romans knew all about this – Camulodunum (Colchester) and the area around Whitstable were known all over the Empire for the quality and flavour of their Native oysters. By the 1860s, more than 700 million of them were being sold a year, mostly at street-corner stalls. Eventually the number of oysters dwindled so much that the government introduced the Pacific oyster, which tastes quite different, to UK waters in 1965 to allow the number of Native oysters to recover. But they struggled to do so. Now they are starting to recover, they're being treated as a delicacy once again.

Most of the fish that's caught on our shoreline goes abroad. When I found that out, I thought, *what the hell is going on?!* A huge proportion of mackerel fished here goes to the Netherlands. I love mackerel – it's actually my favourite fish.

It's such a good fish to barbecue. Thankfully, chefs like Nathan Outlaw and Paul Ainsworth have been flying the flag for British fish and seafood that is adored elsewhere in the world. Like razor clams, whelks, megrim sole and spider crabs, all of which we have in abundance. The shellfish in Scotland is absolutely incredible: award-winning mussels, incredible king scallops, succulent langoustines. But if people don't know about them, they're not going to eat them. Sometimes, a bit of rebranding works wonders, like renaming megrim sole as Cornish sole. I had it in Devon and it's really good. Spider crabs were renamed Cornish king crabs in 2021 and it's already paying dividends. (They taste fantastic.)

British game is incredible and there's lots of it. Venison is one of the most sustainable meats there is and it's also lean and nutritious with less fat than a skinless chicken breast, gram for gram. Deer haven't got any natural predators and numbers are at their highest level in the UK for 1,000 years, which is causing damage to woodland and vegetation. Why not make the most of this rich abundance?

British farmers are growing unexpected fruits, vegetables and plants. Who knew that Isle of Wight tomatoes were so incredible? But then, it's the part of the UK that records the most hours of sunshine, and there's this remarkable valley – Arreton – running through its rural heart that has been used for agriculture for centuries. The guys at the Tomato Stall (with stalls at Borough Market among other places) grow over forty types of tomato in gigantic glasshouses using fertile Arreton valley soil. They've engineered a biodegradable growing system, so all their waste is composted, including the string they use to train the tomatoes, and the compost enriches the soil for next year's crop. They're combining natural abundance with scientific wizardry and the results are spectacular.

Talking of scientific wizardry, the first UK-farmed summer truffle was unearthed in 2015. Plant biologist Dr Paul Thomas had come up with an idea to 'plant' spores of the summer truffle in the root system of trees around the UK in 2009. Six years later, he unearthed a truffle weighing nearly forty grams in Leicestershire. Prince Philip, who was always up for a new challenge, started trying to grow the prized black truffle in his mid-eighties at Sandringham in Norfolk in 2006. And despite the naysayers, twelve years later, he unearthed a crop of them. He was the first person in England to harvest a successful crop of black truffles, also called 'black diamonds' given that they can fetch up to £1,700 a kilogram. Matt Sims unearthed the first Welsh crop of black truffles in 2018 and he now supplies his truffles to the Welsh restaurant trade. I tried some of them on a trip to Wales in 2023 – they are so fresh and full of flavour.

That trip opened my eyes to a breathtaking landscape and some equally breathtaking food. The Beach House in Oxwich Bay – right on the beach – was extraordinary. You go there expecting seafood but the menu showcased all sorts of local Welsh produce. I'd never had laverbread before, but chef Hywel Griffiths's take on it, laced with locally picked seaweed, was a revelation. Then we had lobster, caught in the bay we were sitting in, followed by Hywel's signature dish, Gower Salt Marsh Lamb, served with celeriac, girolles, goat's cheese and a beer vinegar gel. The amazing flavour of the meat comes from the salty shoots the lambs graze on in the marshes and the whole dish went together so well. It was a perfect marriage of flavour, seasonality, provenance and originality, and a testament to the collaboration between farmers, suppliers and chefs, all working together. It was the region on a plate. What they served was familiar but sophisticated food – a defining quality of modern British food.

Which brings me on to Tom Kerridge.

After rising up the ranks to head chef, in 2005 Tom bought a run-down pub with his wife, just like Heston Blumenthal did ten years before. They chose the Hand and Flowers in Marlow, Buckinghamshire, and did it up, with Tom running the kitchen and Beth in charge of front of house. What they did there was remarkable. They transformed a road-side pub on an A-road into the first pub in history to win two Michelin stars. Tom focused on bold, powerful and unpretentious flavours using the best seasonal ingredients. He had a clear vision: to bring British pub food to new heights. Tom had an absolute blinder as Brits would say.

Unlike other cuisines, British cooking did suffer from an identity problem for a long time. If you'd asked most Brits thirty years ago to give some examples of British cooking, they would have answered with familiar pub grub: roast beef, steak and kidney pie, toad in the hole or fish and chips – that sort of thing. Britain had an inferiority complex, hidden in the shadows of its more illustrious culinary neighbours. And maybe part of that was because Britain didn't have a culinary lineage going back generations that they could draw from, unlike France and Spain. Britain was given a helping hand by outside influences, like the Roux brothers, but many of the inspiring figures to have come from within have been curious, intelligent innovators with a passion for history. People like Fergus Henderson and Heston Blumenthal.

When the Michelin Guide was expanded to the UK in 1974, only twenty-five restaurants were awarded one star (for comparison, 624 restaurants in France were Michelin-starred that year). As of 2023, there are 182 Michelin-starred restaurants in the UK, which puts Britain seventh in the world. Over a third of them are listed as 'modern British', 'contemporary British', 'creative British' or 'traditional British'. But it's much more than Michelin Guides. Britain has become a nation of foodies. You just have to look at the farmers' markets that have popped up everywhere since the first one appeared in 1997. Look at Borough Market, near London Bridge – it's exploded in the last twenty-five years since it changed from a wholesale market to a retail one. It started with just a few stalls but now it's a tourist destination. It's a special spot and a hub for like-minded people, whether they have a passion for producing food or for eating it.

Brits are now obsessed with food, food programmes and cookbooks. Jamie Oliver is the top-selling British non-fiction author. The only Brit who has sold more books is J. K. Rowling! He's been so successful abroad too – his books have been translated into over thirty languages. He's an incredible British export and has revolutionised the way people cook food because he's made it so simple and fun to follow. Bish bash bosh and you're done!

The UK is a melting pot when it comes to cooking. Some ingredients, techniques and dishes were brought over by invaders and occupiers, and after they left, Brits decided they were worth whisking up again. The Romans brought over fruits and vegetables that we now think of as quintessentially British, like cucumbers, asparagus, plums, leeks and peas. As mentioned above, Native oysters were only cultivated under the Romans.

Other ingredients and dishes were brought over by migrants. Kedgeree and mulligatawny soup are examples of Anglo-Indian cuisine that became big in the UK in the 1790s. You can't get more British than fish and chips, right? Well, it's likely that the technique for battering and frying fish came from Sephardic Jews who settled in east London in the seventeenth century. As for the chips, the French and the Belgians can keep fighting over that one, but the Brits might well have been the first to bring the fish and chips together. Brits are fantastic culinary curators, finding things we like from other countries and incorporating them into our own culture. Often with magical results.

Brits have discovered they've got an incredible larder and rediscovered how much the sea has to offer. Now they're using both the mix of cultures and the local produce in all sorts of creative, innovative ways. British chefs are bringing their own personality, culture and tradition to their recipes. And they're training another generation of young British chefs who are looking up to these guys the way that chefs in the 1960s and 70s were looking up to the Roux brothers. They're creating their own history. Many of the better restaurants are now working in partnership with suppliers and farmers who are growing quality products. And I've witnessed the change.

During my career in the restaurant business, I've been lucky to travel all around the UK. When we opened Galvin at Windows in 2006, a group of us, including the head chef André Garrett, went on trips around the country to meet producers, try produce and forge relationships with the local industry. One of these trips was to Loch Fyne. I remember tasting incredible langoustines, oysters, mussels and scallops, and learning how they're cultivated. It's also just amazing to see where your food comes from. You each bring inspiration back to the restaurant and start thinking about how you could prepare and cook the produce you've seen. And seeing as you know where it comes from, and you've been inspired by it, you can talk about it to your customers with passion. They trust you because you know what you're talking about. It's not like you're just selling something you've bought frozen from a van. You know the provenance, and that connection really matters.

The more you learn, the more you want to learn. And when you've developed a passion, you'll end up wanting to share it with other people. This is how you instil a new wave of British chefs and hospitality professionals with pride about what they do. I feel we all have a responsibility to educate ourselves and others about that. And it's not just about the restaurant scene – the appetite for greater quality is taking over the whole nation. It's become a movement, a kind of quiet food revolution. I say 'quiet' because I believe part of the reason British food is not more widely celebrated is because Brits don't shout about it. The Brits go about their business in a humble, quiet way. It's part of the charm of the culture. Every fruit matures in its own way, in its own time. British food is doing that now.

But some things don't need to evolve. They're perfect the way they are. When I walked into a British 'caff' for the first time, it was love at first sight. The idea of being able to have breakfast any time between 6 a.m. and 4 p.m. makes perfect sense, especially to a French guy in his twenties who'd been out late and didn't wake up until midday! You don't want to jump straight into lunch – sometimes you just want eggs done sunny-side up on some lovely bread buttered all the way to the sides. And then I discovered the wooden London cabbie shelters, originally built in the nineteenth century and painted that beautiful dark green. There are now only thirteen of them dotted around central London, twelve of which are still in operation. They're no bigger than a horse and cart and you can't sit inside on the little U-shaped table unless you're a cabbie, but you can order through the window hatch.

There's a cabbie shelter in Blackheath that I used to go to that isn't an official cabman's shelter, but loads of cabbies and bikers use it. They don't do a lot of food and drink but what they do, they do perfectly. I say this a lot in my line of work: there's no advanced level in service. It's all about the basics. And the basics are the same whether you're at the Ritz or a roadside café. You've got to deliver what the customer wants, and with a roadside café, if you order a bacon sarnie, you expect soft, fresh bread, buttered with nice, salty butter topped with crispy bacon and brown or red sauce. And a lovely builder's tea on the side. One, two, three, four, five sugars – whatever you want. And it's not just the food you're getting. It's the snappy, cheerful banter with familiar faces both behind the counter and in the queue. No one's taking themselves too seriously and everything's done with a smile. And then you're on your way. Every single time you go, you know the food is going to be consistent and high quality. Like a pub, they're pleased to see you, they remember your name and they remember your order. You can't ask for more than that.

8

'What Britain Does Best (And What Brits Think They Do Best!)'

This chapter isn't so much about what other silly preconceptions the French have about the British, it's more about me capturing what I think the Brits are particularly good at. And it's not really so much about comparing with the French. I think the French are the French and that's the way it is. Gino, on the other hand, thinks that the Italians are the best, and he really means it! In my experience, the Brits tend to be self-deprecating, humble and modest, and if they say 'we're the best' at something, it's almost always tinged with irony or humour. So they need someone foreign to step in and tell them what they genuinely do the best. I'm up for the task.

In 2016, the polling company YouGov took a survey of over 1,000 people in eighteen different countries and one of the questions was 'How do you feel about your own country?' One of the six possible answers was: 'My country is the best in the world.' It might not be a surprise to learn that 41 per cent of the American respondents thought their country was the best, putting the USA at the top of the table. Britain was mid-table, with 13 per cent. So who was bottom? France, with just 5 per cent of French interviewees thinking France was the best country in the world. Amazingly, France was joint top (with Vietnam) for the number answering that their country was the worst in the world! *Sacré bleu!* In a way I'm not surprised because, as we saw in Chapter 3, the French are never happy. France is the most visited tourist destination in the world. We've got some of the best food and holiday spots on earth along the Mediterranean coast, we've got the Alps and the best skiing in Europe, we've got wine regions and regional cuisine with their own gastronomic identities. France can grow its own food and feed itself. We've got history, *châteaux*, beautiful countryside and yet we think it's shit. It's incredible. Why can't we just enjoy it and shut up?!

I think it helps that I've been out of France for over thirty years so I can see it for what it is, both good and bad. I love the deep conversations I know I'll have in France with complete strangers about life, philosophy, politics, history, relationships, sex and love. French people get straight to the juicy bits. They want memorable debates that stimulate, excite and energise them. You feel like living life in the moment and getting something out of your system. To me, conversation is never time wasted. Whenever I set off for Paris, I get butterflies in my stomach because I'm so excited by the endless possibilities. There's a timeless air of romance about

Paris, and gazing over the roofs from Montmartre is one of the best views in the world.

But there are things that exasperate me about the French. As already mentioned, striking is just part of our cultural DNA. So are three-course formal meals and rigid timings. The Brits are more relaxed, fair-minded and patient. Things happen at a gentler pace. Not only have I come to admire these qualities, I've also come to adopt them. It's crept up on me how British I've become.

My brother Pierre has been in the UK for almost as long as I have, and when we chat to each other, we speak in English as much as we do in French. We both weave in and out of the two languages, using the expressions and words we love or find most useful from each. In group chats, we usually speak in English. I actually find it easier to write in English than French, especially on my phone, because the accents are always a bit of a faff. Although English isn't my mother tongue, it lives inside me just as much as French does, maybe even more so because I dream in English. English is simpler in some ways because along with the accents you don't have to worry about nouns having genders. But English is as complicated as you want it to be – there are over 600,000 words in the Oxford English Dictionary compared to just over 400,000 in French. Brits may think that French sounds like the most beautiful language, but English is the richest and arguably the most expressive. I know that sometimes people can move to another country, find an ex-pat community that speaks the same language and end up spending all their time with the ex-pats. It would have been easy to do that when I moved here because the staff at La Tante Claire (and Le Gavroche) were mostly French. But if I'd done that, it would have felt like I was staying on the fringes when I wanted to be in the thick of it. So I completely immersed myself in British culture straight away. That way, I figured I'd enjoy Britain much more. I spoke English all the time and learned new words, slang, expressions and euphemisms every day. I'm still learning them now. I was also listening to snippets of conversations on the streets. I'd listen to the radio, and watch *Only Fools and Horses* and *Monty Python's Flying Circus* on TV. I loved both of them straight away not only because they're very funny, but because I realised that these classics reveal a lot about the Brits. *Monty Python* manages to be both very smart and very silly, never taking itself too seriously. The fact that 'New York, Paris,

Peckham' was on the Trotters' Reliant Robin said as much about the Brits' lovable self-deprecation as it did about Del Boy's permanent state of optimism. I lived in Peckham for many years and so the connection and humour was never lost on me. I found it especially funny asking British friends to translate the 'French' that Del Boy used. 'What on earth does he mean by "Mange tout, mange tout"?!'

Who's the most famous landscape gardener in history? Lancelot 'Capability' Brown. And over 150 of his gardens still survive in Britain. So I'm giving the Brits gardening. You do it the best and you don't give yourself enough credit for it. I'd never heard of an arboretum before I moved here. A garden ... for trees? Recently I found myself watching a documentary about the Victorian pioneer Robert Stayner Holford, who financed plant-hunting expeditions to every corner of the British Empire. It made me realise that the spirit of adventure is at the heart of British gardening. Brits want to explore and experiment. Holford's legacy is Westonbirt Arboretum in Gloucestershire, now known as the National Arboretum. What he created was, like Britain itself, both a stunningly beautiful and wonderfully diverse place.

I think I love gardening because it embodies characteristics about the Brits that I admire so much. It requires patience, creativity, curiosity and a love of nature. It's also about a sense of respectful order and pride in its historical roots. The French approach landscape gardens very differently, and it tells you something about French attitudes in general. Everything is formal, structured, symmetrical and elegant. Also don't step on the grass – it's not for relaxing on! The British, on the other hand, want to live alongside nature, not control it. That idea was at the heart of the English landscape garden, with its romantic wildness, which became the most popular landscape garden style in Europe.

Another craft the Brits have absolutely mastered is making beer. I've been all over the world and I've never been to a country that brews better beer. Both the quality and the variety are second to none. Pale ales and IPA in particular are so full of flavour, character and personality. The French beer market is changing, in part because the French have been inspired by what's been happening on the other side of the Channel. Now you find much more hoppy beers in France made in microbreweries. The French are sometimes resistant to change, but they make an exception if they know that something's really good!

Brits make the best whisky in the world, there's no question. Bourbon's good and so is Japanese whisky, but the original and most impressive is made in Scotland. In March 2024, the world's best single malt at the World Whiskies Awards was made in Norfolk. So Scotch is now being given a run for its money from across the border! It might surprise you to learn that until 2023, when India finally claimed the top spot, the top Scotch whisky importer in the world by volume was ... France. The French love the stuff far more than their own spirits, like cognac or Armagnac.

The Brits love animals. Their empathy and compassion is unmatched. Dogs and cats become more than pets – they're absolutely part of the family. Brits love watching programmes about animals and the ones they make are the best in the world. The dedication, skill, innovation and patience of the teams behind *Blue Planet*, *Green Planet*, *Frozen Planet*, *Wild Isles*, all of them ... is utterly mind-blowing. And nobody else has Sir David Attenborough. There is no figure in France that has that international presence. He's a global ambassador for nature. A national treasure who's earned every one of the thirty-nine initials after his name. He's royalty, really, to the Brits, and like Queen Elizabeth, he's been a constant presence. They've been watching him for all of their lives.

The Brits are the best at talking about the weather. I'm not actually joking here. It's a literary art form. The opening line of Geoffrey Chaucer's *Canterbury Tales* is about 'April showers'. William Wordsworth's most famous line? 'I wandered lonely as a cloud.' When you think of *Wuthering Heights*, you can almost hear the wind on the moors. Shakespeare even named one of his plays after a storm. The Brits don't have the worst weather in the world, not even close. But British writers have made it so epic that you guys think you do. And then, what do you say when it is actually nightmarish weather outside? 'It's a bit blowy today.' Brits win talking about weather hands down. And downplaying disaster!

Of course, I can't not mention Shakespeare again, because he is the finest writer in history. I'm fascinated by him and travelled to the Shakespeare Birthplace Trust a few years ago to meet Stanley Wells, the scholar and honorary president of the trust. Shakespeare pushed the boundaries and that's a common trait in great British works of fiction that were ahead of their time from *Jane Eyre* to *Brave New World*. And then there’s fantasy fiction. The greats, like J. R. R. Tolkien, C. S. Lewis, Philip Pullman and Douglas Adams, are all Brits. And one of the things that unites them is that Britishness runs through each of the lands they created. They also feature underdogs as their protagonists, and that is something that humble, self-deprecating Brits connect with. It’s a recurring theme in British culture. I can’t believe I’m bringing up Agincourt to make my point, especially given that occasionally people mention it and wave two fingers at me(!), but there’s also ‘the Few’: the airmen who won the Battle of Britain, Robin Hood, Harry Potter, Frodo Baggins, even Del Boy. They all won in the end against the odds.

Brits do monarchy the best. When people from abroad think of the UK, often the first thing that comes into their heads is the royal family. Compared to the other monarchies around the world, the British royal family is the one that’s most like a fairy tale. Members of my family in Limoges are fascinated by the British royal family, as are so many others in France. They buy magazines about them, watch news bulletins on them – and nearly 10 million people in France tuned in to watch

Kate and William's wedding. Nine million people watched the coronation of King Charles III, which amounted to 70 per cent of the French audience watching TV at the time. *Le Monde* called it a 'historic day under a perfectly British rain'. They couldn't resist a dig.

The fairy-tale part of the British royal family comes to life with the weddings of William and Harry to non-royals or 'commoners' to use the funny technical term. It's a monarchy that goes back centuries and all the accumulated heritage, traditions and pageantry goes with it. For his coronation, Charles III wore a stunning golden cape that was made for George IV in 1821. He was crowned with St Edward's Crown, which was created for King Charles II in 1661. The fact that all these things have stood the test of time is a testament to how deeply royalty is embedded in the British psyche. When you think about the number of engagements members of the British royal family undertake, you can see how much they're always trying to be close to their people. They want to shake hands and talk to people. Princess Diana was incredible at this and made a real connection with the French people. She was a kind soul who wanted to change things for the better. She was brave enough to stand up for what she believed in and the French admired her courage and resilience and sympathised with her suffering. She was elegant, eloquent, beautiful and there was a sense of mystery about her. There was nothing that the French people didn't like about her.

Nobody does it bigger than the Brits when it comes to royalty, either. They've got all these magnificent castles and estates just like kings and queens had hundreds of years ago when they wielded absolute power. The ones that they do own, like Windsor Castle and Buckingham Palace, are massive tourist attractions, as are the ones that they used to own, like the Tower of London and Hampton Court. You can't ignore the influence the royal family has had on Britain and Queen Elizabeth II played a huge part in this. She was the Queen for as long as people can remember and part of the reason she was so admired was because she was completely selfless in her role. There was no excess, no scandal – she was a shining light that people could look up to. But for me, it was that moment during the London 2012 Olympics opening ceremony that took her legend to another level, when she walked along the Buckingham Palace corridors with Daniel Craig as James Bond (and her corgis) before 'leaping' out of the helicopter and into the London Stadium.

That sealed her legacy because it showed her sense of humour and that she could maintain her regal status while coming down to everyone else's level. I was there, in the stadium, and I couldn't believe what I was seeing. The sense of surprise and jubilation from the Brits around me was moving. It's moments like this that cement that status of the royals in society and keep the fairy tale alive.

London was a fairy tale that summer of 2012. I would cycle from my home in Peckham up to Park Lane during those few weeks of the Olympics. The roads were closed off except for the vehicles transporting the athletes, officials and dignitaries. The city was so clean, and so beautiful. It was the height of summer and no one does summer like Britain. The British summer mirrors the Brits perfectly. Everyone's in a good mood and wants to soak up as much of the sun and good times that are on offer. It's neither too hot nor too cold – it's just right. It feels level, like everything's perfectly balanced. So the countryside looks stunning. It's not like parts of France or Italy which can get too dry and dusty. It's still that magnificent green in the UK with its rolling hills with different shades of green and yellow. It makes me feel so peaceful and calm. There's nothing too big or too dramatic – it's soft and gentle. Everywhere you go in the countryside, there are flowers and gardens and people on picnic blankets.

The British have mastered the art of the picnic. Spending a leisurely lunch in a park or by a beauty spot with your friends and family or watching the sun go down while you eat and drink what you like is a joy to the Brits. The French don't really picnic unless they're stopping during a long drive, or maybe just as an occasional novelty to break up the tradition of sitting at the table and spending several hours over a meal. The French think the table is more comfortable and more civilised. The Brits are much less restricted. You can grab a nice hot Cornish pasty, fish and chips and an ice cream and you'll happily stay at the beach all day. Growing up in Limoges, once in a blue moon, mostly on a Sunday, my mum would make an announcement to the family. 'I don't want to cook today. We're going to eat like the Brits.' And that meant *grab whatever you want from the fridge and sort yourself out*. I bloody loved it.

It felt liberating to 'go British' because the French follow the rules when it comes to dining. In some cases, it's actually protected by law. You can't eat your lunch at your desk in French offices and that rule has been in place since 1894. I think that's a good thing because your brain needs a break. Many offices have canteens where people come together to chat and eat, but lots of people go out to a bistro or restaurant for a three-course meal. Many businesses close between 12 p.m. and 2 p.m. and French people can take up to two hours for their lunch breaks. Sure, some opt for a *jambon-beurre* (a ham and butter baguette), but for most people, they'll have a lovely sit-down meal. Food shouldn't be a means to an end. It has to be enjoyed. And when I'm cooking at home, I never treat food as simple fuel. I must do something that's going to be delicious and will give me pleasure, even if it's just a sandwich. I live for the 'ooohs' and 'aaahs' from people I serve it to. The pleasure I take from cooking starts from the moment I begin thinking about what I'm going to make. There is an element of performance about it and satisfying the senses. Cooking is a way of giving happiness to others and showing them love. We share a beautiful moment together, enjoy a break from life and everyone leaves feeling better.

The Brits started grazing in the nineteenth century, with the invention of afternoon tea. What a unique British creation. It started in 1840 with the Duchess of Bedford, who was upset that dinner times were getting later at the start of the Victorian age. This meant that fashionable ladies were 'peckish' (one of my favourite British expressions) by 5 p.m. She described it as a 'sinking feeling' so she asked for tea, bread and butter and cake to keep the wolf from the door. Afternoon tea became a big social event. Fashionable ladies even had clothes specifically for afternoon tea. We don't have anything like afternoon tea in France. I think it's because of those full three-course meals at lunchtime so we're fine until dinner. In Britain, you guys are always hungry! All the best British hotels do epic afternoon teas. And what better way to pull up outside than in a luxurious British car?

When it comes to making high-end cars, Brits really are the masters. Rolls-Royce, Bentley, Jaguar, Range Rover, Aston Martin – what a list that is. The attention to detail, the luxury, the speed, the comfort – it's all breathtaking. The French used to have a luxury car market, but that all changed after World War II when the government steered the direction of the car market to favour a select number of big firms. The smaller luxury carmakers suffered and never recovered and the French largely became known for building cars that anyone could afford. When I was working in Monte Carlo, in 1990, I'd watch the cars coming up to the casinos. I don't think I ever saw a French car! They were always Italian supercars, like Ferraris and Lamborghinis, or Rolls-Royces, Bentleys, Aston Martins and Jaguars. Those were the cars I grew up fantasising about as a teenager when we were watching James Bond films.

We know that the Brits have the best fictional secret agent, but they also do real-life explorers the best. Russ Cook, aka the Hardest Geezer, really caught the British imagination in 2024. In April, he became the first person to run the entire length of Africa, running almost 10,000 miles – or 377 marathons – in 352 days. He dealt with being robbed at gunpoint and being kidnapped by a machete-wielding gang. The nickname 'Hardest Geezer' makes me laugh because it's both tough and doesn't take itself seriously. It's so wonderfully British, like the first thing he said to the media after he finished, which was: 'I'm a little bit tired.' The art of the understatement again! It's the kind of thing you imagine a nineteenth-century British explorer would say. Having some of the greatest explorers and adventurers in history inspires some of the great British modern-day explorers like Ranulph Fiennes, Bear Grylls, Levison Wood and

Ellen MacArthur. There's a fearlessness, inquisitiveness and curiosity about Brits that I really admire and it's built into British culture.

It's reflected in the fact that in the UK, between school and university, many students choose to go on a gap year. Sometimes they work abroad, but most of the time they're travelling the globe, pushing themselves and learning new things. Maybe it comes from the fact that you live on an island so to get anywhere else you had to be great sailors and navigators. Prince William went to the jungle in Belize to learn survival skills, and built houses and walkways in Chile (and famously scrubbed toilets). Prince Harry worked on a ranch in southern Queensland and helped build a clinic in Lesotho in southern Africa. These examples inspire others from their generation. It still blows my mind that British teenagers are out exploring the world on a shoestring. A gap year isn't a thing in France. There's a spirit of freedom about it that is very British.

I can't not mention the BBC as another uniquely British institution. The BBC is the best at what it does. It has a special connection with France because Charles de Gaulle recorded his famous radio broadcast to German-occupied France in

June 1940 on the BBC, and the BBC also lent its airwaves to the French Resistance – they were allowed to broadcast for five minutes each day, and music was used to send coded messages – so it carries a legacy of respect from the other side of the Channel. At its core, the BBC is about being fair-minded, putting out a balanced argument in a very informed manner with no one taking sides. It feels like a force of good in the world. None of the French broadcasters follow the same editorial principles. The BBC is looked up to around the world and people want to emulate it. Whenever I'm travelling around the world and staying in a hotel, I'll always look up the news on the BBC. It's a source of calm, authoritative and reliable reassurance. It's a national institution.

The other national institution that Britain is most known for is the NHS. The Brits are rightly proud of it and it was amazing to see it feature so prominently in the opening ceremony for London 2012. I think the reason people love the NHS so much is because it's very egalitarian. It doesn't matter who you are or where you come from in the world, you'll be seen by the best in the business and they'll fix you up. The NHS is part of the British DNA and it goes beyond politics. It belongs to the people. For the French, universal health care is treated like a given. They expect it because it's the manifestation of the ideals of the French Revolution, so they don't mind demonstrating for it or against it. They have no love for it or allegiance to it – they just want it to work! If it's not working, they'll complain about it loudly. For the Brits, the NHS isn't something they expect as a right – it's something they're grateful for. Clapping for the NHS during the Covid pandemic epitomised the British spirit. It was about being thankful for the healthcare workers doing their jobs in the most dangerous situation. I thought it was a brilliant, beautiful and moving tribute.

There are some rare subjects where self-deprecation goes out the window for the Brits and I find this both funny and fascinating. There are things that Brits do best and things that Brits *think* they should do best. Quite a few sports fit into this category! The fact that the British either invented or wrote the rules for so many of the biggest sports in the world – boxing, football, rugby, tennis and golf to name a few – means that the British feel a sense of ownership over them. And, understandably, it gives the Brits the sense that they *should* be the best at the things they brought to the world's attention. The trouble is, there's a disconnect with the results on the ground. For some of these sports, like tennis, I think the Brits can acknowledge that they're not the best in the world. But there's still a lot of pride there in the sport. Just ask any Brit which of the four tennis Grand Slams they think is the best, and you'll get a clear, proud answer.

The tennis playing might not be their forte, but everything else about Wimbledon, especially the spectacle and atmosphere there, is just wonderful. The Brits care so much! I've been to Roland Garros in Paris for the French Open in June. It's the beginning of the summer, it's on national TV, and everyone's talking about it. But it doesn't mean anywhere near as much to the French as Wimbledon does to the Brits. First, Wimbledon is played on grass and the Brits love their lawns. The tournament is run by the All England Lawn Tennis and Croquet Club and I'm not sure it's possible to create a posher-sounding club, unless you added 'His Majesty's' at the start. There are floral bouquets everywhere and everyone's tucking in to strawberries and cream. It's the height of the British summer, but if it's raining, Brits keep calm and carry on because, to be honest, they're kind of expecting it. There's an egalitarianism about Centre Court that is unlike any other tournament because there are members of the royal family, film stars, music icons and the super-rich sitting in the royal box, but 500 of the premium tickets are set aside each day for anyone who joins the queue.

The Wimbledon queue is one of the most famous queues in the world, and for each day of the tournament, the queue starts the evening before and people bring tents, camping chairs, sleeping bags, picnics, stoves and Thermos flasks. You even receive an official 'Queue Card' which outlines a 'Queue Code of Conduct'. It's not possible to put together a more British sequence of four words. The whole idea of queuing up overnight and actually enjoying it is completely inexplicable to the French. They wouldn't find any of this experience fun – queuing in a park for hours, eating picnics and takeaway food, socialising with people they don't know and not being able to get a good coffee – it's just not their cup of tea. But to the Brits, the Wimbledon queue is like a little festival. People genuinely have a great time. You hear stories about friendships that started in the queue with people from all over the world. I'm sure people have fallen in love in the queue, and it's effectively become their first date. For all these reasons, Wimbledon is a celebration of all things British. It's a festival of Britain. Wimbledon embodies the values and the spirit of Britishness. And I love how much joy Brits take from it. Brits love to do traditionally British things.

Basically, the Brits do big 'events' like no one else in the world. They've become part of the cultural consciousness. Chelsea Flower Show is incredible – it's the biggest flower show in the world, and it's no surprise it's such a big deal when you consider the sheer number of garden centres you drive past all over the country. There's nothing like the scale, quality or passion in France. The Last Night of the Proms is another national event that is a celebration of Britishness, and, like Wimbledon, people can still queue to get tickets on the day. They come wearing silly outfits, ridiculous hats and waving Union flags. The second half of the Last Night is all British classical classics: 'Pomp and Circumstance', 'Land of Hope and Glory', 'Rule, Britannia!', 'Jerusalem' and the national anthem. You've got the super-rich and Fred Bloggs from Peckham all under the same roof witnessing the same spectacle.

Glastonbury is the best of its kind and features the biggest musical artists on the planet. And even though more than 200,000 people are there, it still retains its eccentricity and quirkiness. Going to Glastonbury is like a rite of passage for young

Brits and tickets sell out almost immediately, every year. I love that it takes place in the Vale of Avalon where King Arthur is said to be buried, because it somehow feels like this epitome of British celebration takes place in the heart of ancient Britain. When the weather's good, it's the best place in the world. When the weather's terrible, there's still no place that anyone there would rather be. Millions watch it on television, as they do for the other national events, like the Proms, the Boat Race, Royal Ascot, the Grand National, Wimbledon and the Chelsea Flower Show.

Britain is full of these incredible venues that are iconic in their field. The Royal Opera House, the Globe Theatre, the Royal Albert Hall, Glyndebourne, Lord's, Wembley, Twickenham and the Royal and Ancient Golf Club at St Andrews. There's also a much more modest venue in Bethnal Green, east London, where you'll find the home of British boxing: York Hall.

As far as boxing arenas go, York Hall is a very small, intimate venue. That's what so amazing about it. The ring is in the middle of the hall, the spectators are close to the fighters, and there's a balcony running around the outside looking directly over the ring. It almost feels like a place of worship. Put all this together and it makes for a really charged atmosphere. It's what you'd call a fighters' arena and it has a unique place in the heart for British boxers. It was the venue of David Haye's first fight, Lennox Lewis has boxed here, as have Joe Calzaghe and Nigel Benn. Carl Froch's first four paid bouts were at York Hall. It's a boxing rite of passage to fight at York Hall. If you're fighting at York Hall, you've made it in boxing. It's the place to be. It's a bit like wanting to play Ronnie Scott's if you're a jazz musician.

I first took an interest in boxing aged ten during the time of the great US middleweights Sugar Ray Leonard and Marvin Hagler. Then Mike Tyson came along in the mid-1980s and blew apart the heavyweight division. But when I moved to the UK in 1992, the most exciting boxers in the world were British. Nigel Benn and Chris Eubank were the best middleweights and they absolutely hated each other. They couldn't have been more different: Benn, a former soldier with incredible punching power, and Eubank, a born entertainer with a chin of granite. In the heavyweight division, Lennox Lewis became WBC champion early in 1993. His second title defence was against Frank Bruno, in October 1993, dubbed 'The Battle of Britain'. It was a great fight and Bruno was leading on the scorecards but he tired and Lewis knocked him out. On the undercard that night was Joe Calzaghe, who'd go on to dominate at both super middleweight and light heavyweight for ten years. He won all forty-six of his fights. The British boxers of the 1990s really caught the imagination of the British public. Frank Bruno was some character and Brits loved him. He seemed destined to be the nearly man, who Brits always identify with – take Tim Henman, for example. But at Wembley Stadium, he outboxed Oliver McCall to take the WBC world title in 1995. At the fourth attempt and against the odds, the British underdog finally did it.

Boxing is a brutal, bloody, aggressive sport but it's also got Britishness running through it. It's not an *anything goes* type of fight – there are strict rules. You wear gloves, you don't hit below the belt, you can't hit from behind, you touch gloves at the beginning of the bout out of respect and there's a referee who will stop the fight if it's clear someone can't continue. Bearing in mind that it's fighting, boxing is surprisingly gentlemanly, and the measure of that is evidenced in the rules, which were written by Welsh sportsman John Graham Chambers, and were endorsed by the Marquess of Queensberry, giving boxing an aristocratic seal of approval. And it appealed to the Brits, who value 'fair play' and like to follow the rules.

I started boxing in 2007 and I wanted to learn from the best in the business, so I showed up at Clinton McKenzie's boxing gym in Herne Hill, south London. Clinton's the former British and European light welterweight champion and a legend who's been in the ring with Sugar Ray Leonard. I went up to Clinton and told him I wanted to learn how to box. He looked me up and down and raised an eyebrow, like 'who's this guy?' He was sizing me up, trying to figure out what my game was. But I was persistent and he trained me up. He's a great fighter and a great thinker and I've learned so much from him. I've also worn a few punches from Clinton in the ring. One time, he caught me with a right hook to the body and I was out of the ring for three months with a broken rib. But I couldn't wait to get back in there. I wanted to learn from my mistakes, improve my technique and become stronger, quicker and smarter.

Boxing is all about the basics. Getting your footwork, stance, head movement and jab right, and working on simple combinations of punches. I never tire of practising them because it's the foundation upon which everything else rests. And you have to couple that physical rigour with focus and self-discipline so you can repeat the same movement perfectly a hundred times or more. I love that boxing challenges you mentally as well as physically. It's a space in which training, preparation, concentration, confidence, self-belief and fitness all come together (or not as the case may be!) in a test of strength, skill and stamina.

I go into a boxing bout with a strategy and it's up to me to see if I can keep that up. Sometimes you have to adapt very quickly, because as Mike Tyson famously said: 'Everybody has a plan until they get punched in the mouth.' You have to master fear, because even though you're in a controlled setting with rules, fear can overcome you, especially when you're fighting someone you know is a superior opponent. I go in there to win and I don't want to leave anything in the ring. So I go into a fight thinking 'I'm not going to lose – you're going to have to win!'

Boxing is a great way to keep fit, and I also keep in shape with my daily workout ritual. I started doing fifty press-ups a day not long after I turned forty. Gradually I added more reps to it and, at some point, I settled on 301. It was a good number and it meant I could do sets of thirty, with one for luck. It takes me about ten minutes to complete but sometimes I'll really push myself to do it faster and I can get it down to about five minutes. The press-up is a complete workout for the whole of your upper body as well as your bum and the tops of your legs. So if I just do press-ups and squats, for example, for a twenty-minute workout, I'm set for the day. And the great bonus is I can do it anywhere, which works perfectly because I travel a lot for work and to support my daughter Andrea wherever in the world she's competing. Come to think of it, I might have done more press-ups and squats in hotel rooms than anyone else in the world! I kept it up in the jungle for *I'm a Celebrity*, doing my 301 press-ups, along with 100 squats and 100 reverse squats. I get that it might seem tedious, in terms of repeating the same thing every day, but I don't see it that way because, like I discovered with surfing in Newquay, it's about entering a place of calm inside your head.

I learned how to surf on Fistral Beach and I loved everything about it right away. I enjoyed the way that you're out there early in the morning and that it wakes up your body, sets you up for the day, rids your body of tension and works off the meal from last night. You have to be up for the challenge because it really takes it out of you, even just trying to stand up at first. You keep getting battered by the waves but you keep trying. I loved that it was really difficult and that you've got to combine the skill, anticipation and knowledge to catch the wave. Then it's about the technique and balance to stay up on the board, which is really tough but it's so much fun. You have to be in good physical condition to catch a wave and you've got be a strong swimmer too because otherwise you're just going to be catching the waves near the shore, which isn't as exciting as the ones that are further away and more difficult to catch. You get more pleasure that way. And when you're standing up and you're in control, you suddenly feel like you're the king of the waves. It made me feel like Patrick Swayze in *Point Break*, which was still very much in my mind that first time on Fistral Beach, given that it had only come out two summers before. After you come back to shore, you feel like you've earned your trip to the pub for a nice pint of pale ale and a lovely roast, or fish and chips by the sea. And that always makes you feel good. I like working hard, and I like playing hard too.

To surf, you really need to focus – there's nothing else you're thinking about except catching and surfing a wave. You're not worrying about anything else. So, effectively, that takes you to a place where you're meditating. And that's very refreshing and relaxing for the mind. It gives me a great sense of satisfaction. If you focus on one thing and you can do it well, it's almost like you're having a holiday away from the other cares of the world. You feel like you've been cleansed of all the toxins from your body and mind. The blood's pumping, the endorphins are flowing, and you feel strong and positive.

I enjoy being active, staying fit and feeling strong. It started as a teenager, when I was skinny and self-conscious, so I decided to do something to change it. But I went about it by concentrating on cardiovascular exercise like running, football and handball. I wasn't doing any strength training so I didn't really gain any muscle. It was when I got to around twenty-three or twenty-four in London and discovered triathlons that things started to change. I was training in a way that helped me to bulk up a bit – bulking up within the frame of my body. I was never a big gym guy, though. I was swimming a lot so my shoulders, chest and core were all quite developed. I cycled everywhere I needed to get to in London, however far, so my legs became more powerful.

I used to run to work from where I was living in Peckham. You see all the colours of the city that way, from the industrial Old Kent Road, through to Elephant and Castle, across Westminster Bridge, past Big Ben and on to St James's Park. St James's Park is a bit like Disney imagined what a park would look like, with the magnificent plane trees and the bridge across the lake. Horse Guards Parade is in one direction and Buckingham Palace in the other, and I'd run past the palace, heading through Green Park and then on to Hyde Park. It's so pleasing how all these beautiful green spaces lead into each other – you can almost forget you're in a city.

Sometimes, when I'd go running at the weekend, I'd be gone for three or four hours. I was getting high on adrenaline, endorphins and fresh air. It felt like I was rocket-powered, flying through the streets and parks of London and not letting up until I got back to my house. I discovered a lot of London that way. I loved to run through the City at night after work. The Barbican felt like a modern-day castle, running through corridors, up and down steps, past fountains, beside churches and alongside the London Wall, the old Roman defences with its arches and old gateways. Sometimes I'd run from Bermondsey to Richmond along the river. I'd run come rain, wind, snow or sunshine, day or night. I'd even on occasion run to work in the morning and back home after finishing at the restaurant at 1 a.m. I was fit enough, motivated enough and had enough energy to do it. I became a kind of urban gazelle. When it was just me and the road, I'd get a kind of thrill. It was almost like I was swallowing the road up – it felt as if there was nothing I couldn't do. That's the intensely powerful positive effect running has on your brain. You also have that constant sense that you're bettering yourself. I'm getting fitter, physically stronger and mentally tougher. On top of that, it's an amazing way to see new places. *How far can I push myself?* I would wonder. I was curious to see how far I could go, while feeling the blood pumping through my veins and the oxygen flowing. It was so exhilarating. The adrenaline rush that sport provided was intense and addictive – I couldn't get enough of it. It was the same with dancing.

Sometimes, a few of us would head to Trade nightclub in Clerkenwell after work, listening to house and techno all night. Tony De Vit was one of the resident DJs then and I loved that guy. He even played twelve-hour sets a couple of times. At that time, I was so committed to exercise that I wasn't drinking alcohol, because I didn't want anything to affect my workouts. So I'd turn up at Trade in my shorts and wearing my running rucksack. It was one of those rucksacks that you could fill with water or Lucozade, which kept me going through the night. I'd get high just on the endorphins from dancing. My adrenaline was surging so much it felt like I was surfing the music. I'd dance until 4 a.m., have a quick breather and then go back and dance until 7 a.m. It was glorious madness. And I was still full of energy when the club closed. So I'd run home.

I remember going back home to Limoges over the summer and playing Tony De Vit's music really loud on the record player. My dad sprinted upstairs, shouting: 'The vinyl is scratched, the vinyl is scratched!' trying to yank the disc off the player. 'What are you doing, Dad?!' I said. 'It's not scratched – this is the best bit!' I still play Tony De Vit's music a lot when I'm driving and whenever I put on 'Make Love to Me', I just keep turning up the volume but it can never be loud enough. That track transports me back to Trade and I still feel the exhilaration now, just writing about it. Music has that remarkable quality of wrapping itself around a memory of a time and place, so as soon as you hear the track start up, you go from 0 to 60 in a heartbeat. And then the beat kicks in and you feel like you're taking off, and you keep going higher and higher as the music builds. You don't come back down to earth until it's over. But it would never be over with Tony De Vit, because he'd mix into something else so you just kept flying for hours and hours.

As soon as 'Football's Coming Home' starts up, so does the optimism that this tournament is finally *the year*. England goes absolutely football-mad. The only people that aren't excited are the restaurant owners. When England are playing in the World Cup or the European Championships and they advance further into the tournament, it's a disaster for restaurants, because everyone's in the pub! To be fair, the French get pretty animated about the Euros and the World Cup. The French love beating the Germans as much as the English do. I remember watching the 1982 World Cup semi-final between France and Germany – it was an incredible match, with four goals in extra time levelling the scores at 3–3. The Germans won the shootout (England isn't the only team that loses on penalties to the Germans!) and advanced to the final. But that semi-final is remembered more for one of the most shocking fouls in the history of football. The German goalkeeper, Harald Schumacher, completely took out French defender Patrick Battiston, who'd been put through on goal by the French captain Michel Platini. Battiston was knocked unconscious, lost two teeth, broke his jaw and damaged several vertebrae. It was grievous bodily harm. But the referee didn't even award a foul. After the match, when Schumacher was told about the extent of the injuries to Battiston's face, he said: 'I'll pay for the crowns.' It caused a major diplomatic incident.

Sport has that unique power to unite a nation. You can't help but feel pride when your flag-carrier appears in the opening ceremony. As for Great Britain, you guys are fourth in the all-time Summer Olympics Medal table behind the USA, Russia/Soviet Union and Germany. You're better than France who, just for the record, are in sixth. In the history of the Olympics, there are five sports where Britain sits at the top of the medal table. Sailing (that makes sense), triathlon (Britain has dominated since it was introduced in 2000), polo, tug of war(!) and cricket, which only featured once, at Paris 1900 (although it's coming back for Los Angeles 2028). That was actually the only game of cricket at the Olympics ever played, and it featured

England against France. Amusingly, the 'French' team included just two Frenchmen. The other ten were English!

I get so excited about the Olympics. I'll happily watch any sport because you're getting to witness the best in the world at work. Being the father of an Olympian who's competing at Paris 2024, I'm filled with respect for all the athletes because I know how hard each of them will have trained to get there. Paris 2024 will be the Olympics I'm most emotionally invested in. Andrea's in the form of her life and keeps winning medals. I'm already counting down the days to the opening ceremony. But in terms of pure spectacle and pride in the land that I call my home, London 2012 was unique. I was working at the Hilton on Park Lane at the time and it was the official hotel of the International Olympic Committee (IOC). Every dignitary and VIP from the IOC was staying there and eating in the restaurant, so we had incredible access to the people involved in the event. I was proud to be part of the team that was displaying the UK to the world and showing what modern Britain was about. To be representing the UK was a very special experience.

I was lucky enough to go to the opening ceremony and it was utterly spectacular – the energy in that stadium of 80,000 people was unlike anything I've ever experienced. It was Britain at its best. There were some moments I'll treasure for ever. Everything came together and Britain shone in front of the whole world. Its multiculturalism, its heritage, its achievements – everything was on show and it was a triumph. I thought it was the best Olympic Games that I'd ever seen. I'm French, not British, but I thought: 'We are the best. Nobody can do it better than us!'

Epilogue

My children are half-French and half-Italian but they're 100 per cent British. When they speak French, Andrea and Matteo Lucien speak with an English accent. It's something my mum and my dad, who are *so* French, find quite funny. My kids definitely have a British sense of humour – they're self-deprecating, sarcastic and take the mickey out of me constantly. They are forever correcting my English pronunciation and giggling about it. I'll often say to them: 'Let me remind you that I've been speaking English since before you were both born!' They take the piss out of me gardening and how seriously I treat it. They find it hilarious that I spend so much of my time hunting weeds and that I talk to my garden, saying things like: 'If you're not a plant, you're not allowed to live here!' They laugh at how much I like admiring my handiwork from the National Trust-style bench I've placed in exactly the right position to catch the most of the sun, with a place next to me on the bench for my Earl Grey tea. They think I'm an old-timer. At the same time, they'll joke about anything I buy that they think is too young for me. You can't win, can you?!

Andrea's already got a five-year plan mapped out. I never had anything like that. At twenty, I left France for the UK on what I imagined would be an adventure. It just turned out to be the adventure of my life. The only plan I had was to work in the Premier League of restaurants. I wanted to be one of the star players, go all the way to the top in my chosen profession and be the best that I could be. But I didn't really know how to go about it. I figured it out along the way. I knew that I had a strong work ethic, determination, vision, focus and application. Resilience is something you can only develop when you fall. You don't plan for things going wrong or imagine how you're going to pick yourself up, but I learned to keep going while being true to my vision and my values. I am proud of what I've achieved. I've worked really hard in some of the best places in Britain and with the best people. I've been lucky to be rewarded with almost all of the awards that you can win in the hospitality industry in the UK. Could I have done better? For sure. I've made lots of mistakes. With the gift of hindsight, there are things I might have done differently, but the path I've followed is the one that's led me to where I am now. And when I look at the jigsaw that is my life, I think it all fits and it makes sense. Some of the pieces are French and some are British.

When I first arrived here, it didn't take long to realise that the French are more rigid than the Brits. They like to do French things and stick to them. They like to visit the same places. And if you love all of those things, as my parents do, then you'll find nowhere better. But I need variety in my life. I embrace things that some people might think are completely mad. But there's method in my madness. I like exploring new places and experiencing new things. I don't like to stay still. And, in Britain, I've found a place that feels like me: it's constantly changing.

There was a time when I thought that the French and the British were like chalk and cheese, but we're not that different. We're more like two different types of cheese on a plate – a nice, ripe Brie and a good, strong Cheddar – you can't really compare them directly but you want a bit of both in your life, don't you? Again, *vive la différence*. I've been here for over thirty years and I'm still learning things about the Brits that surprise and delight me. But when it comes down to it, we all aspire to the same things – we want our children to be happy, we want our country to prosper and we want to do well in life. We just have different ways of going about it. The Tricolore and the Union Jack aren't so dissimilar – they're the same colours, just in a different arrangement. I think the differences make us attractive to each other. They also make us laugh. It's a bit like being married. We know each other's strengths and weaknesses so well. We know how to push each other's buttons. But we can also keep each other on our toes and bring the best out of each other.

The reason why Britain appealed to me when I first came here, aged fourteen, was because I knew I'd found a place where anything felt possible. I still feel that way. Britain has an open-mindedness which means that opportunities open up. You just have to have a bit of faith, apply yourself and go and do it. I am so proud to live here. When I visit France, I see it through the eyes of a Brit – I feel like I'm going on holiday. When I arrive back in Britain, I feel like I'm coming home.

ACKNOWLEDGEMENTS

Special thanks to my agent Grant Michaels, to Ben Dunn and Katy Follain

A NOTE ON THE TYPE

The text of this book is set in Linotype Sabon, a typeface named after the type founder, Jacques Sabon. It was designed by Jan Tschichold and jointly developed by Linotype, Monotype and Stempel in response to a need for a typeface to be available in identical form for mechanical hot metal composition and hand composition using foundry type.

Tschichold based his design for Sabon roman on a font engraved by Garamond, and Sabon italic on a font by Granjon. It was first used in 1966 and has proved an enduring modern classic.